THE AFRO-AMERICANS

The Peoples of North America

A THE FRO- AMERICANS

Howard Smead

CHELSEA HOUSE PUBLISHERS
New York   Philadelphia

Cover: The family of John Baptist Ford, a Pullman porter, sits for a group photograph in 1924, the year Ford was chosen by one of his passengers, a Dartmouth College professor, to lecture on his profession at the Tuck School of Administration and Finance at Dartmouth.

CHELSEA HOUSE PUBLISHERS
Editor-in-Chief: Nancy Toff
Executive Editor: Remmel T. Nunn
Managing Editor: Karyn Gullen Browne
Copy Chief: Juliann Barbato
Picture Editor: Adrian G. Allen
Art Director: Maria Epes
Manufacturing Manager: Gerald Levine

The Peoples of North America
Senior Editor: Sam Tanenhaus

Staff for THE AFRO-AMERICANS
Associate Editor: Abigail Meisel
Copy Editor: Nicole Bowen
Deputy Copy Chief: Ellen Scordato
Editorial Assistant: Theodore Keyes
Picture Research: PAR/NYC
Assistant Art Director: Laurie Jewell
Senior Designer: Noreen M. Lamb
Production Coordinator: Joseph Romano
Cover Illustration: Paul Biniasz
Banner Design: Hrana L. Janto

5 7 9 8 6

Library of Congress Cataloging in Publication Data
Smead, Howard.
  The Afro-Americans / Howard Smead.
    p.   cm.--(The peoples of North America)
  Bibliography: p.
  Includes index.
  Summary: Discuss the history, culture, and religion of the Afro-Americans, their arrival in North America, and their acceptance as an ethnic group.
  ISBN 0-87754-854-4
       0-7910-0256-X (pbk.)   AC
  1. Afro-Americans--Juvenile literature. [1. Afro-Americans.]
I. Title. II. Series.
E185.S575 1989
973'.0496073--dc19   88-20300
                                         CIP

Contents

THE PEOPLES OF NORTH AMERICA

CHELSEA HOUSE PUBLISHERS

A
NATION
OF
NATIONS

Daniel Patrick Moynihan

The Constitution of the United States begins: "We the People of the United States . . ." Yet, as we know, the United States is not made up of a single group of people. It is made up of many peoples. Immigrants from Europe, Asia, Africa, and Central and South America settled in North America seeking a new life filled with opportunities unavailable in their homeland. Coming from many nations, they forged one nation and made it their own. More than 100 years ago, Walt Whitman expressed this perception of America as a melting pot: "Here is not merely a nation, but a teeming Nation of nations."

Although the ingenuity and acts of courage of these immigrants, our ancestors, shaped the North American way of life, we sometimes take their contributions for granted. This fine series, *The Peoples of North America*, examines the experiences and contributions of the immigrants and how these contributions determined the future of the United States and Canada.

Immigrants did not abandon their ethnic traditions when they reached the shores of North America. Each ethnic group had its own customs and traditions, and each brought different experiences, accomplishments, skills, values, styles of dress, and tastes in food that lingered long after its arrival. Yet this profusion of differences created a singularity, or bond, among the immigrants.

The United States and Canada are unusual in this respect. Whereas religious and ethnic differences have sparked intolerance throughout the rest of the world—from the 17th-century religious wars to the 19th-century nationalist movements in Europe to the near extermination of the Jewish people under Nazi Germany—North Americans have struggled to learn how to respect each other's differences and live in harmony.

Millions of immigrants from scores of homelands brought diversity to our continent. In a mass migration, some 12 million immigrants passed through the waiting rooms of New York's Ellis Island; thousands more came to the West Coast. At first, these immigrants were welcomed because labor was needed to meet the demands of the Industrial Age. Soon, however, the new immigrants faced the prejudice of earlier immigrants who saw them as a burden on the economy. Legislation was passed to limit immigration. The Chinese Exclusion Act of 1882 was among the first laws closing the doors to the promise of America. The Japanese were also effectively excluded by this law. In 1924, Congress set immigration quotas on a country-by-country basis.

Such prejudices might have triggered war, as they did in Europe, but North Americans chose negotiation and compromise, instead. This determination to resolve differences peacefully has been the hallmark of the peoples of North America.

The remarkable ability of Americans to live together as one people was seriously threatened by the issue of slavery. It was a symptom of growing intolerance in the world. Thousands of settlers from the British Isles had arrived in the colonies as indentured servants, agreeing to work for a specified number of years on farms or as apprentices in return for passage to America and room and board. When the first Africans arrived in the then-British colonies during the 17th century, some colonists thought that they too should be treated as indentured servants. Eventually, the question of whether the Africans should be viewed as indentured, like the English, or as slaves who could be owned for life, was considered in a Maryland court. The court's calamitous decree held that blacks were slaves bound to lifelong servitude, and so were their children.

America went through a time of moral examination and civil war before it finally freed African slaves and their descendants. The principle that all people are created equal had faced its greatest challenge and survived.

Yet the court ruling that set blacks apart from other races fanned flames of discrimination that burned long after slavery was abolished—and that still flicker today. The concept of racism had existed for centuries in countries throughout the world. For instance, when the Manchus conquered China in the 17th century, they decreed that Chinese and Manchus could not intermarry. To impress their superiority on the conquered Chinese, the Manchus ordered all Chinese men to wear their hair in a long braid called a queue.

By the 19th century, some intellectuals took up the banner of racism, citing Charles Darwin. Darwin's scientific studies hypothesized that highly evolved animals were dominant over other animals. Some advocates of this theory applied it to humans, asserting that certain races were more highly evolved than others and thus were superior.

This philosophy served as the basis for a new form of discrimination, not only against nonwhite people but also against various ethnic groups. Asians faced harsh discrimination and were depicted by popular 19th-century newspaper cartoonists as depraved, degenerate, and deficient in intelligence. When the Irish flooded American cities to escape the famine in Ireland, the cartoonists caricatured the typical "Paddy" (a common term for Irish immigrants) as an apelike creature with jutting jaw and sloping forehead.

By the 20th century, racism and ethnic prejudice had given rise to virulent theories of a Northern European master race. When Adolf Hitler came to power in Germany in 1933, he popularized the notion of Aryan supremacy. "Aryan," a term referring to the Indo-European races, was applied to so-called superior physical characteristics such as blond hair, blue eyes, and delicate facial features. Anyone with darker and heavier features was considered inferior. Buttressed by these theories, the German Nazi state from

1933 to 1945 set out to destroy European Jews, along with Poles, Russians, and other groups considered inferior. It nearly succeeded. Millions of these people were exterminated.

The tragedies brought on by ethnic and racial intolerance throughout the world demonstrate the importance of North America's efforts to create a society free of prejudice and inequality.

A relatively recent example of the New World's desire to resolve ethnic friction nonviolently is the solution the Canadians found to a conflict between two ethnic groups. A long-standing dispute as to whether Canadian culture was properly English or French resurfaced in the mid-1960s, dividing the peoples of the French-speaking Quebec Province from those of the English-speaking provinces. Relations grew tense, then bitter, then violent. The Royal Commission on Bilingualism and Biculturalism was established to study the growing crisis and to propose measures to ease the tensions. As a result of the commission's recommendations, all official documents and statements from the national government's capital at Ottawa are now issued in both French and English, and bilingual education is encouraged.

The year 1980 marked a coming of age for the United States's ethnic heritage. For the first time, the U.S. Census asked people about their ethnic background. Americans chose from more than 100 groups, including French Basque, Spanish Basque, French Canadian, Afro-American, Peruvian, Armenian, Chinese, and Japanese. The ethnic group with the largest response was English (49.6 million). More than 100 million Americans claimed ancestors from the British Isles, which includes England, Ireland, Wales, and Scotland. There were almost as many Germans (49.2 million) as English. The Irish-American population (40.2 million) was third, but the next largest ethnic group, the Afro-Americans, was a distant fourth (21 million). There was a sizable group of French ancestry (13 million), as well as of Italian (12 million). Poles, Dutch, Swedes, Norwegians, and Russians followed. These groups, and other smaller ones, represent the wondrous profusion of ethnic influences in North America.

Canada, too, has learned more about the diversity of its population. Studies conducted during the French/English conflict showed that Canadians were descended from Ukrainians, Germans, Italians, Chinese, Japanese, native Indians, and Eskimos, among others. Canada found it had no ethnic majority, although nearly half of its immigrant population had come from the British Isles. Canada, like the United States, is a land of immigrants for whom mutual tolerance is a matter of reason as well as principle.

The people of North America are the descendants of one of the greatest migrations in history. And that migration is not over. Koreans, Vietnamese, Nicaraguans, Cubans, and many others are heading for the shores of North America in large numbers. This mix of cultures shapes every aspect of our lives. To understand ourselves, we must know something about our diverse ethnic ancestry. Nothing so defines the North American nations as the motto on the Great Seal of the United States: *E Pluribus Unum*—Out of Many, One. ⚭

Sharecroppers face eviction in Missouri in about 1935.

A HEROIC HERITAGE

Of all the peoples who have journeyed to America from foreign lands, Afro-Americans have the saddest yet most inspiring story. Unlike immigrants of every other nationality and race, the Africans arrived on our shores naked and in chains. They came as captives, sold into involuntary servitude by European slave traders and their reluctant partners, local African rulers. European slave merchants—who first arrived in Africa in the 16th century—eventually brought a total of approximately 15 million slaves to New World colonies in Central and South America, to the "sugar islands" of the West Indies, and, finally, to North America.

In 1619, British colonists located in Jamestown, Virginia, purchased America's first African workers, 20 in all. These arrivals were not slaves but indentured servants. The African population in America remained tiny until the turn of the 18th century, when Virginians began importing slaves from West Africa at a rate of about 1,000 per year. By that time slavery had spread throughout the colonies. Africans worked as field hands in the South and as domestic servants in the North. From 1776 to 1783, slaves bolstered the ranks of George Washington's army, as Americans waged their War of Independence against the British. In fact, a 47-year-old slave, Crispus Attucks, earned a place in revolutionary history by leading colonial forces during the Boston Massacre in 1770.

The revolutionary era was a promising time for slaves. In 1783, for example, a Massachusetts court granted liberty to Quork Walker—a slave who claimed the right to freedom on the grounds that the preamble to the state constitution declared all men "free and equal." That year, Massachusetts prohibited slavery. In 1784, Connecticut, New Jersey, and Rhode Island followed suit.

At the very same time, however, blacks in the American South were about to suffer a major setback. In 1793, Eli Whitney invented the cotton gin, a machine that revolutionized the nation's cotton industry, which became the backbone of the economy in the South. During the first decade of the 1800s, cotton exports nearly tripled—from 30 to 80 million pounds—and the demand for slave labor escalated quickly on the large farms, or plantations, of the South.

At the same time, an antislavery movement—called "abolitionism"—gained momentum in the North. Abolitionists launched a crusade, and many lost their lives in sectional conflicts that divided the nation from about 1820 until the start of the Civil War in 1861. The abolitionist movement not only catalyzed the Civil War, but also spawned a new generation of black leaders.

The most influential of these leaders was Frederick Douglass, a freed slave who became an eloquent voice for the Afro-American community. His autobiographical work *Narrative of the Life of Frederick Douglass*, published in 1845, remains an important document of slave conditions and one of the classics of American literature. As the racial climate changed, Douglass served as a barometer of Afro-American feelings. He joyfully welcomed the emancipation of slaves and later expressed horror at the racist backlash that denied to blacks the hard-won gains of the Civil War. Shortly before his death, in 1895, he told a group of whites, "The rich inheritance of justice, liberty, prosperity and independence, bequeathed by your fathers is shared by you, not by me. The sunlight that brought light and healing to you, has brought stripes and death to me. The Fourth of July is yours, not mine. You may rejoice, I must mourn."

By 1890 the promise of freedom won during the Civil War had soured, as yet another form of oppression took root in the South, where a block of racist legislation known collectively as "Jim Crow" laws forced Afro-Americans into second-class citizenship. Worse than these unjust laws was the covert sanction southern states gave to violence unleashed against blacks. Throughout the 1890s, whites shot, burned, and lynched blacks at an alarming rate; an average of one black was killed every two and a half days. Like the fugitive slaves of an earlier generation, Afro-Americans fled north to safety, but in far greater numbers. In only 10 years, from 1910 to 1920, nearly 1.5 million blacks escaped the South.

In the North, most Afro-Americans settled in urban enclaves and together forged a new identity as city dwellers. In the 1920s, New York City boasted the largest and grandest black neighborhood in the nation: Harlem. Here more than 200,000 blacks lived and worked together, creating a vibrant culture—the Harlem Renaissance—alive with gifted poets, novelists, painters, and performers. Another metropolis, Chicago, emerged as the mecca of black music. There, ragtime, blues, and Dixieland merged to form one of the century's great art forms, jazz.

Hard times hit in 1929, when the Jazz Age crashed into the Great Depression, which lasted through the 1930s. This economic crisis put millions of Americans on breadlines, but Afro-Americans suffered the most. Yet the very bleakness of the decade spurred blacks in a new direction—toward social reform. In 1937, for instance, black train porters banded together to form their own union. Buoyed by this success, black labor leaders galvanized the community to change its second-class status.

Afro-Americans were thus ready to defend their rights in the 1940s, when the nation's fortunes changed again, this time as a result of World War II. The war effort opened up lucrative job opportunities in the booming factories that supplied weaponry to the U.S. Army. But blacks, though desperate for work, were ignored by employers. Instead of mutely accepting this

A studio portrait of Frederick Douglass, taken in 1856.

injustice, black union organizer A. (Asa) Philip Randolph pried open the doors of the all-white defense industry in 1941 by threatening to stage a mass protest in Washington, D.C. Randolph's bold move paid off. The U.S. Congress passed legislation that outlawed job discrimination.

This triumph set the stage for one of the most stirring chapters in American history, the civil rights movement of the 1950s and 1960s. Protests in strongholds of Jim Crow such as Birmingham, Alabama, and Albany, Georgia, drew widespread attention to the plight of Afro-Americans. Their struggle for justice aroused the sympathy of the nation and thrust into international prominence a young black preacher, Martin Luther King, Jr., who in 1964 was awarded a Nobel Peace Prize.

But as blacks made gains, dissension arose within the civil rights community. Some leaders found King's method of nonviolent protest too tame; others thought the movement should shift its focus from the South and its institutional (or *de jure*) segregation, to the North, where blacks had legal rights but were locked into ghettos and locked out of decent housing and jobs. Malcolm X, Stokely Carmichael, and others argued that white Americans would never give blacks a fair shake and that the minority community must strengthen its own economic and political base independent of the larger society.

The civil rights movement became splintered and nearly collapsed in the mid-1960s, when a rash of rioting broke out in American cities such as Los Angeles, California, Detroit, Michigan, and Newark, New Jersey. Blacks and whites squared off in mobs that left peaceful cities in ruins. The crisis culminated in 1968, when King was assassinated in Memphis, Tennessee, at the age of 39.

For the next two decades black leaders struggled to fill the vacuum left by King's death. Yet Afro-Americans continued their drive for equality and made some gains, especially on the political front. By the early

1980s, many large cities had black mayors. Blacks also made an impact on national politics. Two congressmen, for example—Charles Rangel of New York and William Gray of Pennsylvania—ranked among the leaders in that legislative body.

The late 1980s saw the emergence of the most remarkable political figure of all, the Reverend Jesse Jackson, who in 1988 ran a highly successful campaign for the Democratic presidential nomination. For the first time, Americans of all descriptions—including whites long mired in racism—voiced their belief that an Afro-American deserved to occupy the highest office in the land. Jackson ultimately lost the nomination—to Massachusetts governor Michael Dukakis—but his campaign caused an entire nation to reassess its prejudices.

Afro-Americans continue to excel, too, on another front—culture. Black dance troupes, such as the Dance Theatre of Harlem and the Alvin Ailey American Dance Theater, delight audiences around the world because they encapsulate America itself, its energy, passion, and humor, its willingness to improvise new forms. The same is true, to an even greater degree, of Afro-American music. Americans have blacks to thank for jazz, blues, rhythm and blues, rock 'n' roll, and rap. These forms have added sparkle to our own culture and have helped create the international myth of American glamor.

Today, most Americans acknowledge the tremendous contributions of the black community, but many obstacles still bar the way to true equality. An alarming percentage of blacks remain trapped in the ghetto, with its shabby housing, dismal schools, broken homes, teenage pregnancies, and rampant drug culture. Many Afro-Americans hurdle these obstacles only to face the subtle racism of employers, landlords, and—most disappointing of all—the framers of public policy. Blacks can draw strength, however, from the legacy of their forebears, whose capacity for hope finally overcame the cruelty of their oppressors. ✎

In 1979 Andrew Young, then U.S. ambassador to the United Nations, defends his meeting with the Palestinian Liberation Organization, a terrorist group not officially recognized by the United States.

A limestone relief dating from about 1370 B.C. shows the head of an African taken prisoner.

FROM FREEDOM TO SLAVERY

The story of the Afro-Americans begins not on this continent but on another approximately 4,800 miles away: Africa, a vast land mass of nearly 12 million square miles. Most ancestors of today's Afro-Americans lived in West Africa. This region, located on the northwestern coast of Africa, had a highly diverse population. More than 250 languages were spoken there, all subgroups of the three major West African tongues: Sudanic, Bantu, and Hamitic. The region's culture was equally varied. Different communities practiced distinct customs and developed unique civilizations. In fact, hundreds of years before the discovery of America, three great empires—in the countries of Ghana, Mali, and Songhai—flourished on the grasslands south of Africa's Sahara Desert.

It was in this region that slave trade began at the end of the 15th century. It was initiated by European countries, which had recently entered an age of exploration that led them to colonize foreign lands in North and South America—the New World. The competition to annex new territories became especially fierce between two seafaring powers, Spain and Portugal, which raced to establish settlements across the Atlantic. By 1494, relations between the two nations had grown so strained that Pope Alexander VI issued the Treaty of Tordesillas. It provided for Spain's control of all of

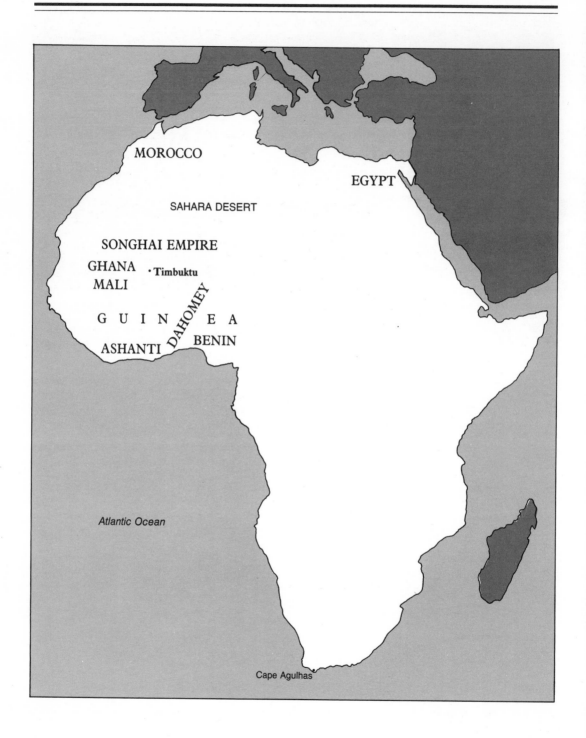

MOROCCO

EGYPT

SAHARA DESERT

SONGHAI EMPIRE

GHANA · Timbuktu

MALI

G U I N E A

DAHOMEY

ASHANTI BENIN

Atlantic Ocean

Cape Agulhas

South America save for Brazil, which fell under the sovereignty of Portugal. So did Africa. In this era, Portugal started trading with African tribal chiefs. At first the Portuguese coveted gold and ivory. But over the next 50 years, their interest shifted toward another precious natural resource, human beings, to fill a growing need for free labor in the burgeoning colonies of the New World. African traders willingly obliged the Portuguese because slave trade enabled them to dispense with people whom they viewed as undesirable, particularly warriors taken captive during battles with enemy tribes and nations.

As time wore on, the demand for human beings escalated. It could not be satisfied by the small supply of wartime prisoners African chiefs had been offering. The Europeans threatened to take their business to rival tribes, and Africans began hunting slaves with the sole intention of selling them to whites for a profit. Soon African traders grew dependent upon the slave trade and were easily manipulated by the Europeans, who

Spanish explorer Fernando de Soto terrorizes a tribe native to Florida in this 16th-century engraving. The cruelty of the Spanish toward indigenous peoples of the Americas led to the outlawing of Indian slavery by the Spanish Crown and the importation of African slaves to take their place.

This bronze figurine of a Portuguese slaver was made in the West African kingdom of Benin during the 16th or 17th century.

used every available means of increasing the slave supply.

One ruse was to exploit the hostilities that often put tribes at odds with each other. For example, Europeans armed the Dahomeans—a people from the Guinea coastal territory first called the Kingdom of Benin, later known as the country of Nigeria and now called Benin—with enough weaponry to conquer and capture neighboring adversaries. The Dahomeans balked at the plan, but when the Europeans threatened to transfer their loyalties to the enemy tribe, the Dahomeans became hopelessly ensnared in the slave trade, delivering other Africans to whites in order to save themselves from enslavement.

African slave traders, known as *caboceers*, captured their victims singly, in small groups, or in large numbers, but in every case they sought those best suited for the rigors of the New World—healthy males and females between the ages of 18 and 35, although some children also were captured. Sometimes slavers were outnumbered by their prey, but they generally had superior weaponry and could overpower their victims, whom they chained together at the ankle or wrist or linked at the neck by a wooden yoke. Thus bound, the captives then embarked upon a grueling march—sometimes as long as 600 miles—to the coast, where European ships awaited them. Not all the prisoners made it. Some resisted their captors and were killed. Others died from the rigors of the trip. A lucky few managed to overpower their captors or simply slipped away.

Once they reached the coast, the tired and bewildered Africans were stripped naked and penned into *barracoons*, or stockades. But the worst of their ordeal lay ahead of them—the harrowing voyage to the New World aboard slave ships. These ships lay at anchor until their holds had a full cargo of slaves. Then the "middle passage" got under way. This term referred to the second leg of a three-part trading system. The first part began when European ships—first Portuguese, but mostly British after the 18th century—sailed to Africa bearing manufactured wares. Cotton textiles, pewter, gunpowder and guns, whiskey, and boxes of beads went to Africans who, in return, handed over slaves. Next came the second step—the middle passage—whereby Europeans shipped the captive Africans across the Atlantic to the West Indies. There the slavers traded their human cargo for sugar, which they took back to Europe, completing the final part of the journey.

The Atlantic Crossing

For the captives, only the middle passage mattered, and it was a nightmare. The Atlantic crossing took four to eight weeks, and for its duration women, men, and children were crammed into tightly packed quarters in the "between decks" of a vessel, located below the main deck and above the cargo hold. The ceiling of this area usually reached no higher than five feet and ran the length of the boat. From the side of the ship, rough wooden planking extended six to nine feet toward the center. This planking formed the slaves' quarters for the entire journey. There were no mattresses, no sheets, no blankets, no pillow—just hard wood. During storms

Captured Africans—shown in a European engraving— begin the long trek toward slavery.

A joint work by American lithographers Nathaniel Currier and James Merritt Ives depicts the branding of slaves on the coast of Africa.

or rough seas the slaves sustained numerous cuts and scrapes.

A typical slave ship had two or three such shelves, which held a total of up to 700 people. The space between them never exceeded three feet. Only the smallest children had room to sit up. Bound in pairs by the wrists and ankles, the male slaves occupied the longest shelves, filling the center of the vessel. Each shelf had two or three buckets for the slaves to use as toilets. If a slave was too cramped or too weak to maneuver the bucket under himself, he relieved himself where he lay and had to lie in his own excrement. The buckets often spilled or were knocked over during the night, further befouling the already stifling conditions. The sick generally languished in their own corner. But those who suffered from ill health rarely made it to the New World. An English clergyman named John Newton, writing in 1750 about the slave trade, commented, "Every morning, perhaps, more instances than one are found of the living and the dead fastened together."

The wretchedness of the slaves' existence was worsened by the monotony of their days. If weather permitted, the crew brought the slaves on deck at about 8:00 A.M. They fastened down the men, either by attaching their leg irons to ringbolts set into the deck or by chaining them to the gunwales, the upper edges of the boat's side. Women and children could roam freely. At 9:00 A.M. the slaves ate their first meal, usually boiled rice, millet, or cornmeal, sometimes flavored with a few lumps of salted beef. The fare might also include starchy vegetables such as plantains, yams, or manioc, an edible root. The slaves washed down their meals with half a pint of water, drunk out of a pannikin, a small, hollowed-out pan rather like a large deep spoon.

The ordeal was so demoralizing that slaves often sank into a condition known as suicidal melancholy or fixed melancholy. A slave so afflicted lost the will to live, slipped into a deep depression, and died. According to one eyewitness, "Notwithstanding their apparent

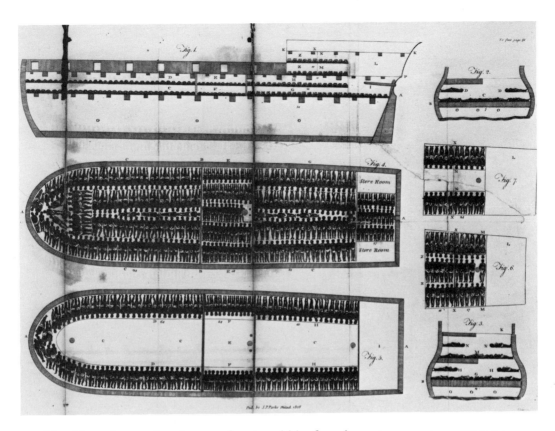

good health each morning three or four would be found [dead]. One of the duties of the slave-captains was when they found a slave sitting with knees up and head drooping, to start them up, run them about the deck, give them a small ration of rum, and divert them until in a normal condition." Some slavers hired a musician to play a drum, banjo, or even a bagpipe in order to boost the spirits of the slaves. Others merely directed a sailor to beat out a crude rhythm on an upturned kettle.

Another practice was "dancing" the slaves. After breakfast, chained men were dragged on deck where they stood in their fetters and exercised either by hopping in place or by jangling their arms and bodies. The crew walked among them with cat-o'-nine-tails making sure they complied with this forcible recreation, a process meant to keep the slaves "healthy" in body and mind.

An engraving published in Philadelphia in 1808 diagrams the packed interior of a 19th-century slave ship.

While the slaves "jumped in their irons," crew members went below to carry out the sickening task of cleaning out the slave quarters, a job performed no more than three times a week. They scrubbed the fouled planking with stiff brushes and hot water, scraped and swabbed the deck, then dropped red-hot iron pellets into bowls of vinegar to freshen the sour air. The captain had to maintain strict discipline to make sure his crew performed this onerous job. If he relaxed his rule or if the seas were rough or the slaves rebellious, the task went undone.

After dancing the slaves and cleaning out "'tween decks," the sailors served the second and final meal of the day at about 3:00 or 4:00 P.M., a healthful but unappetizing mixture of boiled horsebeans—the cheapest food available in Europe—mixed with flour, palm oil, water, and malagueta pepper, a spice obtained on the African coast. The sailors themselves found the mixture disgusting and derisively referred to it as "slabber sauce." Their revulsion was shared by the slaves, who often refused to eat their food, instead throwing it at the crew or at each other. When the meal ended, the slaves returned below to their planked shelves.

An illustration from the book Revelation of a Slave Smuggler *(1856) dramatizes a scene in the hold of the ship* Gloria.

Slaves could escape this grim routine only by taking their own lives, an option they sometimes chose over enslavement. But slavers, seeking to protect their investment, did all they could to prevent suicides. If vigilant crew members restrained the captives from jumping overboard, the slaves often fell into such despair they tried to starve themselves to death. Many received severe beatings for refusing to eat, a form of passive resistance that became so widespread that European slavers invented an instrument—called a *speculum orris*—used to force-feed those who fasted. This device operated like pliers in reverse and enabled slavers to pry and hold open a slave's mouth so the slavers could pour food into it through a funnel. Slavers frequently discouraged self-starvation by shoving hot coals down a slave's throat; the victim died but served as a warning to others.

Often slaves who retained their will to live and who ate died anyway, either from the diseases that ravaged the slave ships or from suffocation due to lack of oxygen in the air between decks. The filthy living conditions on board bred pestilence; in fact, the crewmen fell ill and died more often than the slaves themselves. Dysentery—caused by slaves' wallowing in their own filth below deck or by eating with soiled fingers—claimed lives on nearly every voyage and often led to bloody flux, a dreaded condition in which slaves excreted blood and mucus.

Flux was widely feared, but it inspired less terror than another ailment, smallpox, an incurable virus that afflicted crew and slaves alike. Smallpox doomed whomever contracted it. If the illness itself did not claim the victim's life, he would perish as a result of the practice—common on board slave ships—of throwing overboard anyone bearing its symptoms, a drastic method of avoiding contagion.

Slaves were tossed into the sea not only to halt epidemics but also to decrease the weight of a ship. For example, if winds were not blowing, the crew sometimes jettisoned part of its cargo in order to gain speed

European sailors jettison slaves in this woodcut created in about 1750.

on the waves. This practice originated during the first transatlantic voyages of the Spanish, who pitched their horses overboard when they reached the doldrums—an area of the mid-Atlantic known for its listless winds and currents. Slave ships followed suit by sacrificing not horses but human beings.

This practice was so widespread that slave merchants took out insurance—from Lloyds of London and other companies—that covered the eventuality of jettisoning some or all of their human cargo. The British were still jettisoning slaves as late as 1781. That year the *Zong,* after completing an arduous middle passage lasting 3 months and 16 days, jettisoned 132 slaves within sight of Jamaica, their destination. The ship's insurance company agreed to pay the merchants £30 for each dead slave, but an English court found the payment illegal and stated "that a higher law applies to this very shocking case." After this decision, the practice of jettisoning slaves, by British slavers at least, came to an end.

In any case, it benefited the slavers to deliver their cargo not only intact but, if possible, in good health. Often they promoted a false appearance of robustness in the slaves in order to fetch a higher price at the market. They fattened their captives by feeding them all the remaining food left on board and by keeping them on deck, where there was fresh air, as long as possible. Slavers also tried to disguise any sign of disease. Someone suffering from the bloody flux had his anus plugged with candle wax. Other afflictions, such as yaws (a tropical disease marked by ulcerating lesions), running sores, or scrapes, were concealed with a mixture of gunpowder and iron rust. Slavers also oiled the bodies of the slaves to highlight their muscles.

Once in port, a ship's captain might arrange for the sale of slaves himself, but usually that chore fell to factors, slave traders who received a commission on each sale of 15 percent per slave plus a smaller percentage of the total proceeds. Factors sold slaves either individ-

A copper engraving details the auctioning of slaves on the coast of Africa.

ually or by lot. The most profitable deals were made when the owner of a large sugar plantation—or a group of wealthy planters—bought an entire cargo of newly arrived slaves. The most barbaric of all sales venues was the auction block, though only the choicest slaves—those who were already "seasoned" by years of servitude or those born in the Americas—underwent this indignity.

In general, planters bought inexperienced slaves in large lots. Sometimes they bid "by inch of the candle," a process whereby factors lit a candle and took offers on the slaves until the wick had burned down an inch. But most Africans were sold in "the scramble," so called because at the sound of a cannon shot, the planters or their agents scrambled about the stockade attaching a handkerchief or colored ribbon to the slaves they wanted to purchase. In some cases the scramble took place aboard the ship.

These rites of sale officially marked the end of the abominable middle passage, but not of the slaves' sufferings. Ahead lay a life of bondage to the slave master and his subordinates. ∾

*Four generations of a slave
family pose for a photographer
in Beaufort, South Carolina, in
1862.*

SLAVERY

During the more than 350 years of the slave trade, most of the 15 million Africans arriving in the Western Hemisphere were put to work in South and Central America and in the sugar islands of the West Indies: Cuba, Hispaniola (an island now shared by the countries of Haiti and the Dominican Republic), Jamaica, and Puerto Rico.

In 1619, a Dutch merchant ship unloaded 20 Africans in the English colony of Jamestown, Virginia—the first to set foot in North America. These early arrivals were not really slaves, however; they eventually earned enough laboring in the tobacco fields to purchase their freedom, in the manner of indentured servants. After several decades the demand for workers exceeded the supply, and Virginians turned to the slave trade. They did not buy slaves fresh from Africa. They preferred slaves who had already logged some time in the West Indies, where previous owners had already broken them into the rigors of slavery. North American colonists also favored "Creole" slaves, American-born children of African parents. Not until the 18th century did British colonists begin large-scale importation of slaves directly from Africa.

Although slaves became commonplace in the South, they played a far more limited role in the northern colonies, where they generally lived in cities. Things changed after the American Revolution, when merchants from the cities of Boston, Massachusetts, Newport, Rhode Island, and Philadelphia, Pennsylvania, began importing Africans to the New World. Northern slaves usually performed household duties or were rented out by their owners to work in urban shops and factories.

King Cotton

Slaves never became an integral part of the North's industrial economy; the region produced no cash crop that required a large permanent labor force. In the South, however, slavery grew into a major institution. In the 1600s and 1700s, slaves had raised tobacco in Maryland, Delaware, and Virginia, and along the Carolina coast they cultivated rice and indigo, a plant used to make dye. In the 19th century, the need arose for thousands more slaves in a new industry, the cotton trade, which revolutionized the economy of the South.

First domesticated in Africa, cotton cultivation spread to the Middle East and India before the Christian Era and had long been a significant force in the world economy. Two types of cotton grew in the American South. Long-staple or long-fiber cotton—used in the production of fine lace—flourished in the islands off the Georgia coast, but nowhere else. A heartier plant, short-staple cotton—also known as green-seed, piedmont, or upland cotton—grew easily throughout the Deep South, from Georgia to east Texas.

At first short-staple cotton seemed unsuitable for mass production because its short fibers made the removal of seeds by hand an extremely difficult task. This problem was solved—and the slaves' hopes of freedom ended—in 1793, when northerner Eli Whitney invented the cotton gin, a machine designed to separate cotton fiber from seeds, hulls, and foreign matter. Whitney's simple machine, which he patented in 1794, used teeth to comb the cotton through a grating, thereby leaving the troublesome seeds behind. It allowed cotton to be cultivated on a grand scale—an endeavor requiring widespread labor.

As cotton agriculture spread, slavery spread with it, from the Tidewater states of Maryland and Virginia to the Georgia and North Carolina Piedmont into south-

Slaves in South Carolina prepare cotton for the gin.

western Virginia. Soon Tennessee and new U.S. territories acquired under the Louisiana Purchase of 1803—including Mississippi, Alabama, Louisiana, and Arkansas—began importing slaves to cultivate cotton. Plantation owners, aided greatly by the cotton gin, grew rich from the fibers of this plant.

The cotton gin was not the only invention that spurred the American cotton industry. The textile industry in England—the largest importer of U.S. cotton—had already benefited from the automation of weaving, made possible by such innovations as the water-powered loom and the spinning jenny, a machine that could spin 8 to 11 strands of cotton simultaneously. This invention and others elevated cloth making from a cottage industry to a factory enterprise.

These developments boosted English imports of cotton from the American South. In 1790 merchants in Richmond, Virginia, exported 30 small bags of cotton. But after the cotton gin was invented, exports rose sharply to 30 million pounds in 1800 and rose again to 80 million pounds by 1810. Cotton had become king in the South.

This growth depended entirely on the labor of slaves. Their population in the South more than quadrupled from 700,000 in 1790 to 3.2 million in 1850 and rose still higher to 4 million in 1860. By the eve of the Civil War, three-fourths of all the slaves in the United States produced cotton.

This enormous population of slaves was owned by only 385,000 whites. They represented some of the wealthiest and most powerful people in American society, including 12 of the nation's first 16 presidents. Most slave owners held fewer than five slaves. But the planters—who by definition possessed 20 slaves or more—owned most of the slaves in the South. By 1860, 25,000 planters owned 2 million slaves between them, an average of 80 each.

The Slave Codes

Slavery was an institution, and as such a complex set of rules developed to regulate it. In the colonial era, "slave codes" severely restricted the legal rights of slaves. Codes prohibited enslaved blacks from participating in lawsuits, from testifying in court against whites, from owning property or firearms, or from possessing alcohol. Most slave states did not recognize slave marriages, and many prohibited slaves from learning to read and write in order to make them even more dependent upon their owners and thus forestall rebellion.

Laws also limited religious practices. Whites generally had to approve the choice of preachers, and the preachers themselves could not freely address their congregations. Again, the fear among whites was that churches might become cradles of revolt. Slave codes set up a system of armed patrols that guarded against insurrection and apprehended runaway slaves. Under these laws any white person could stop any black person he encountered and demand to see either proof of freedom or the pass that all slaves had to carry when they left the plantation. These regulations reduced even the 250,000 free blacks living in the South to second-class citizenship.

Plantation Life

The basic unit of cotton production was the plantation. The largest of these sprawling farms were located in Louisiana, the Mississippi Delta, the Alabama Black Belt (so-called because of its rich black soil), and coastal

Black country churches, such as this one in Louisiana, were a mainstay of many slave communities.

South Carolina. Plantations also sprang up around Natchez Trace, a 449-mile commercial route linking the cities of Natchez, Mississippi, and Nashville, Tennessee. In some plantation counties, slaves outnumbered whites by more than two to one. Other counties had no slaves at all. Many white Southerners went through their entire lives without ever laying eyes on a slave. Yet slavery was the foundation of southern society.

On plantations, slaves performed various jobs and held different ranks. For example, slaves who became skilled carpenters, blacksmiths, and coopers enjoyed greater privileges than the majority, who worked in the fields. Field slaves were usually divided into gangs of 5 to 10, supervised by a slave driver, usually a slave himself, who was held accountable for the performance of his gang.

In addition to field slaves, drivers, and artisans were those who belonged to another class altogether—the house servants. A large plantation might include a domestic staff composed of two entire families, who held the posts of maid, cook, butler, and gardener. The "mammy" served as governess, taking charge of the owner's children. She teamed up with the butler, generally her husband, to oversee the other servants.

Afro-Americans sit outside the remains of slave quarters in Florida, in the late 19th century.

With the exception of the domestic slaves, who worked directly for the planter and his family, all others answered to an overseer, in almost every case a white man hired by the planter to keep the slaves in line. The master allowed the overseer to handle discipline and punishment, which could be severe. Overseers became hated figures among slaves.

Field slaves lived on a subsistence level, surviving on a minimum of food, clothing, and shelter. Most slave cabins had a dirt floor, one window covered with a burlap flap, and an opening rather than a doorway in the front. These shabby quarters were aligned in rows. At the end of the rows stood a larger dwelling, which housed the overseer. The cabins were situated near to the manor house but hidden from the line of vision of the planter and his family.

The cabins were crudely furnished with a table, perhaps one or two chairs, and a single bed where parents and the smallest children slept. The rest of the family slept on the ground on mattresses filled with hay, grass, or straw. The cabins let in rain and wind and provided little warmth during the winter, which in the cotton regions was mercifully short.

Slave codes required planters to issue each male slave two shirts, two pairs of trousers, and a pair of shoes each year. Women received one or two dresses. The children wore hand-me-downs and went barefoot. Food rations were even stingier. Most codes stipulated that slaves receive a weekly ration of a peck (about eight quarts) of cornmeal and three to four pounds of salt pork per family. Slaves supplemented their diet by growing their own vegetables, trapping game, and, when they were permitted to do so, fishing.

The treatment slaves received from their masters varied tremendously. Some owners were brutal sadists who worked their slaves mercilessly and threatened them with corporal discipline so painful it amounted to torture. The whip was the most common means of punishment on plantations. Most slaves—men and women alike—felt its stinging heat or the imminent possibility of it at least once in their life. Masters instructed their overseers to use the whip whenever necessary to quell restlessness among the slaves or to enforce discipline. Instead of whipping slaves en masse, the overseer usually singled out one unfortunate victim as an example to the others. One whipping of a rebellious slave effectively instilled terror in the rest. A slave had no protection from this mistreatment because the law considered him another man's property, not a human being. When a slave suffered a whipping, he could not take his master to court nor could he fight back with his fists.

Overseers on large plantations used the whip more frequently than did small farmers who owned five slaves or less. But the whip was not the only means of enforcing discipline. For example, a master might extend work hours beyond the normal limit (slaves usually worked dawn to dusk during much of the growing season, but did not have to labor for half of Saturday and all of Sunday). The master sometimes bribed his slaves into good behavior by rewarding them with gifts of extra clothing or food or by offering them a special holiday or an extra day off per month if the slaves raised their individual quotas.

Masters also manipulated the slaves' private lives. They knew they valued their bonds with one another above anything else. Because many slaves had loved ones on neighboring plantations, a master often denied weekend visitation passes as a punitive measure. Even more to the slaves' disliking, he might refuse to sanction their marriages as a means of enforcing discipline. Most slave codes outlawed slave marriages, but it was not at all uncommon for a master to ignore this law and permit his slaves to wed. Some masters encouraged matrimony in the belief that it promoted stability and happiness. But even if a master allowed his slaves to marry, he often threatened to break up these unions by selling one of the spouses and separating the couple for life.

The master also retained his authority by restricting the slaves' right to practice religion, one of the chief comforts of their life. Yet, even the most merciless masters realized that religion played a central role in the slave community and could not be stamped out altogether. In essence, Afro-American religion blended Christianity with the faiths indigenous to West Africa. This hybrid creed taught that the law of God was superior to the law of man and thus gave slaves spiritual independence from the whites who controlled their daily lives.

Masters usually reserved the right to choose who preached to their slaves and the contents of their sermons, often prescribing pious sermons about such topics as brotherly love and the rewards of the afterlife. But slave communities greatly preferred black preachers who drew on the great oral traditions of their African forebears to develop a powerfully rhythmic style of oration. These preachers delivered a gospel of liberation. They interpreted the tenets of Christianity to emphasize the importance of freedom, dignity, and self-respect. The churches they organized—the earliest of which predated the Civil War—encouraged the black quest for independence from white control.

Slave Culture

Christianity represented just one aspect of the culture slaves developed in their plantation communities. Only recently have historians come to recognize the sophistication of slave culture, which they long believed had been thoroughly inhibited by the hardships of servitude. Nothing could have been further from the truth. Within their quarters, slaves developed an independent culture unknown to their masters. The slave community, for instance, included its own—benevolent—figures of authority whom the others looked up to, men and women of great integrity who offered hope in the face of the overseer's bullwhip. Enclosed slave societies gave their members a group identity that enabled them, in the words of black historian Nathan Huggins, "[to] hold together through deep trauma and adversity. . . . slaves laid claim to their humanity and refused to compromise it, creating families where there would have been none, weaving a cosmology and a moral order in a world of duplicity, shaping an art and a world of imagination in a cultural desert."

One testament to the richness of slave culture survives in its folktales. Forbidden by law to read and write, blacks spun fantastic spoken narratives that passed from one generation to the next. These fables expressed the slaves' own aspirations for a better life by describing how small, seemingly weak animals (who represented the slaves) defeat larger beasts (the slaves' hated owners). The most popular stories centered around either the adventures of the small but sly Brer Rabbit or the triumphs of a slave named John or Jack, who ingeniously outwitted his oafish white master.

Slave Families

At the core of slave society was the family, and slaves struggled valiantly to maintain this vital institution. If the master prohibited slave marriages, blacks conducted their own ceremonies in secret, often drawing on the traditions of West Africa. For example, instead of taking their vows in a church, slaves jumped over a broom, a ritual that can be traced back to their homeland. Couples usually created two-parent households, although circumstances often tore them apart: About one-third of all slave families unraveled when one member was sold to another plantation. Owners usually kept women and children together, selling off the father or the sons. On the well-established plantations, black families had a better chance of remaining intact—some endured for three or four generations.

The emphasis slaves placed on the family lent dignity to relations between the sexes. But sometimes wedlock proved impossible, as, for example, when lovers lived on separate plantations. In these cases, the slave community usually tolerated intimate relations between the couple. This tolerance was not extended to adultery.

The community also objected fiercely to the sexual favors planters and overseers often demanded of slave women. This form of abuse was outlawed under slave codes, but whites often disregarded the law and took

Toussaint L'Ouverture, known as the George Washington of Haiti, stands in military dress in a 19th-century engraving.

young female slaves as their mistresses. The offspring of these liaisons lived as slaves and were usually accepted into the slave community.

Slave Rebellions

Although family life, religion, and folk tales softened the horrors of slavery, they did not lessen the humiliating fact of servitude, and slaves sought more direct means of resisting their bondage, either through violent rebellion or through subtle and covert acts of resistance. Wherever there were slaves in the Western Hemisphere, there were slave revolts. The success of these uprisings varied greatly from region to region, depending on several factors.

Slaves stood a better chance of freedom if their region had places to escape to, such as dense jungles or rugged mountains. They also fared better if the region's slave population exceeded that of owners; if the slaves rebelling were African-born and shared a common ethnicity; if plantations were large and produced only a single crop; and if the owner resided far from his plantation and visited infrequently. In addition, slaves were more likely to stage a revolt if the slave-holding society lacked cohesiveness. This combination of circumstances occurred most frequently in the Caribbean, a region whose blacks developed a proud history of armed resistance.

Fugitive West Indian slaves, known as maroons, established independent societies in several Caribbean islands, including Jamaica and Haiti. Throughout the 1700s, Jamaican slaves fought full-fledged wars against planters and eventually united under Cudjo, a maroon leader. From 1733 to 1738 Cudjo masterminded a guerrilla war against the vastly superior British army, winning 1,500 acres of land for his people. In 1791 Cudjo's counterpart in Haiti—Toussaint L'Ouverture—helped rid the island of European domination by organizing other maroons into a standing army of several thousand troops. His decisive victory against the French army stunned European and American slaveholders alike and made him a national hero among Haitian blacks.

Perhaps the most successful maroon society was the Republic of Palmares, founded deep in the Amazon jungle of Brazil in 1605. According to historian John Hope Franklin, "Palmares was a remarkable political and economic achievement for the fugitive slaves of Brazil . . . it grew into a complex political organism of many settlements of which Cerca Real do Macaco was the capital." At its height, Palmares boasted 20,000 inhabitants who traded with nearby towns and lived peaceably within a system of law. Although Palmares fell to a European invasion in 1695, stories of its success reached slaves in many other communities, including those in the American South. Centuries after Palmares disappeared, slaves told tales of the great maroon kingdom that had thrived for nearly 100 years.

The First Stirrings of Rebellion

Slaves did not enjoy similar success in the United States, where the total number of organized revolts equaled only a fraction of those staged in Central or South America or the Caribbean. Despite repeated defeats, American slaves never became resigned to their lot. Since the time of the American Revolution, slaves in the United States fought on plantations and also in courts of law in order to end their bondage.

In fact, slaves made great headway during the revolutionary era. Their first triumph came in 1783 when Quork Walker sued his master for his freedom on the grounds that the preamble to the state constitution declared all men "free and equal." The court ruled in his favor and in its decision ended slavery not only for Walker, but for all blacks in Massachusetts. The Walker case set a legal precedent and several New England slaves successfully won their freedom in the courtroom, victories that ultimately led to the abolition of slavery in the North. But the trend of freeing slaves traveled no farther south than Virginia. In 1831 the Virginia legislature came within one vote of abolishing the institution of slavery.

The liberation of northern blacks can be traced to the important role they played during the revolutionary war. In 1770, for example, an escaped slave named Crispus Attucks led the attack on British troops in what became known as the Boston Massacre, shouting, "The way to get rid of these soldiers is to attack the main guard!" Some historians consider Attucks the first man to die in the American Revolution.

During the War of Independence, many slaves volunteered to fight against England and received their freedom in exchange for military service. This arrangement aided the revolution by supplying rebel troops with auxiliary soldiers and by countering a similar offer from the British, who also needed an infusion of men into their forces. Thus, at the end of the war many former slaves lived as free men. The Revolutionary era offered blacks the best conditions they would know until the Civil War brought about the abolition of slavery.

American Slave Revolts

Once the booming cotton industry reinforced slavery in the South, blacks staged just four revolts, only two of which gained any momentum. The first occurred in 1800 in Richmond, Virginia, under the leadership of a slave name Gabriel Prosser. Gabriel's Revolt was secretly planned for months. It involved 1,000 slaves, all of whom had organized into a small fighting force, armed with guns, pikes, scythes, and bayonets. The rebel slaves met six miles outside of Richmond, intending to capture the city and to occupy it until the state legislature guaranteed that slavery would be outlawed. The plan was foiled when a slave betrayed the plot to authorities. Virginia governor James Monroe led the local militia out to meet the slaves and to turn them back. No battle ensued, but the leaders of the uprising, including Gabriel Prosser, were arrested and executed.

In 1811 the least-known but largest slave revolt in American history took place in St. John-the-Baptist Parish, Louisiana, just outside New Orleans. The revolt included some 500 slaves who had been brought to Louisiana by their French colonial masters, who were themselves refugees from the Haitian slave revolt. After arriving in North America, these slaves escaped, armed themselves, and marched on New Orleans with drums beating and flags flying. The militia, much better armed, rode out to meet them and attacked. Although the slaves fought bravely, they had no chance of winning and the militia triumphed.

Eleven years later in Charleston, South Carolina, Denmark Vesey, a slave who had purchased his own freedom, organized a plot among slaves to seize the city and ransom it in exchange for an end to slavery. Vesey devised a complex scheme to kidnap government leaders. On the eve of the revolt, however, a slave disclosed the plot to whites, and Vesey and his coconspirators were arrested. South Carolina authorities apprehended 131 slaves in all and hanged 37, including Vesey.

The best-known slave revolt in U.S. history occurred in 1831 in Southampton, Virginia. It was led by a plantation headman named Nat Turner, who rose up

An illustration from A Popular History of the United States— *published in about 1880— portrays the arrest of slave insurrectionist Nat Turner.*

in revolt with other slaves and killed his master and the master's family. These slayings initiated a wholesale slave insurrection that progressed from one plantation to another as slaves murdered their owners and liberated each other. Turner's uprising led to the deaths of about 60 whites and included among its participants approximately 70 slaves. The rampage was halted when federal and state troops crushed the rebellion and captured and executed Turner.

Slave revolts were just one means by which slaves in the South offered resistance to their bondage. Because outright rebellion posed great dangers for them, slaves employed more subtle means of protest. For example, slaves would covertly and purposely break plantation machinery or would set fire to a barn—acts that disrupted the daily life of the plantation and thereby lightened their own burden.

The slaves' prime target was the overseer. When this hated figure drove slaves especially hard or otherwise mistreated them, they sometimes resorted to outright murder. More often, slaves tried to sabotage the overseer, either by getting him drunk on corn liquor, a staple in the slave quarters, or by informing the master, through one of the house servants, that the overseer had committed an indiscretion.

When all else failed, slaves ran away. Between 200 and 300 slaves escaped every year, most of them from the upper South and the border states. In all, some 60,000 slaves escaped to free territory. They usually journeyed north via one of two routes: through eastern Maryland into Delaware and Pennsylvania or through western Maryland and across the Mason-Dixon Line—the border between Pennsylvania, a free state, and Maryland, a slaveholding state—into central Pennsylvania. Sometimes slaves followed trails farther west, such as those along the Mississippi or Ohio rivers, that led them north.

The vast majority of slaves ended their flight in Canada, where slavery had been outlawed by the mother country, England. Canada was much more enlightened about slavery than the United States. Canadian law not only admitted runaways into the country; it also denied entry to professional slave catchers—poor whites known as "patty rollers"—sent to track the blacks down.

The United States, in contrast, granted federal assistance to slave owners trying to recover their slaves. In 1793 Congress passed the Fugitive Slave Law, which made it a criminal offense for a citizen to harbor a fugitive slave or to prevent his or her arrest. A second piece of legislation—the Fugitive Slave Act of 1850—increased sanctions against aiding runaway slaves. Nowhere in the United Sates, not even in the antislavery North, could runaway slave be completely safe from capture and re-enslavement.

Slave-state legislatures feared political pressure from antislavery groups would seriously damage the "peculiar institution," a euphemism used by some apologists for slavery. By 1860 the slave codes had become so tyrannical that it was nearly impossible even for willing masters to *manumit*, or free from bondage, their own slaves. The only recourse the master had was to obtain passage of a special act by the state legislature, a process that cost time and money.

In any case, few slaves relied on the kindness of masters. Instead they plotted their own journey to freedom. Many who succeeded did so by escaping along a series of trails and paths collectively known as the Underground Railroad. This secret route from the South to the North was led by "conductors," brave men and women who sneaked into slave territory to guide runaway slaves out of bondage. The most famous conductor was Harriet Tubman. She had escaped from a Maryland plantation in 1849 and at great risk to her own safety—a bounty had been put on her head—returned to the South as many as 19 times to lead slaves on the Underground Railroad. She alone escorted 600 slaves to freedom, including her sister, both her children, and her mother and father.

Tubman plotted these escapes down to the smallest detail. She preferred to start her journeys on a Saturday night because owners could not print newspaper announcements of runaways until Monday morning, and the time in between gave her a headstart. Tubman had great sympathy for enslaved blacks, but none for cowards. If one of her party lost his nerve, Tubman pulled out the pistol she always carried and then threatened to kill him with the words "live free or die." She also brought along a small vial of tincture of opium, a sedative for crying babies, when slave catchers lurked nearby.

Harriet Tubman was just one of many men and women known as abolitionists because they worked to abolish slavery. They viewed the peculiar institution as immoral and unchristian and could not comprehend how Americans, who were steeped in the tenets of their Declaration of Independence, could sanction the enslavement of human beings in their midst. The abolitionist movement attracted members of both races, including the prominent journalist William Lloyd Garrison, who published the *Liberator*, the leading antislavery newspaper of the day.

Underground Railroad conductor Harriet Tubman (far left) poses with some slaves she led to freedom.

THE LIBERATOR.

VOL. I.]   WILLIAM LLOYD GARRISON AND ISAAC KNAPP, PUBLISHERS.   [NO. 33

BOSTON, MASSACHUSETTS.]   OUR COUNTRY IS THE WORLD—OUR COUNTRYMEN ARE MANKIND.   [SATURDAY, AUGUST 13, 1831.

The vast majority of abolitionists, however, were blacks. Many made their home in the North and worked as clergymen. Others, like Frederick Douglass, an escaped slave who held several government-appointed posts after the Civil War, published abolitionist newspapers such as the *North Star*, named after the star that guided conductors on the Underground Railroad. Douglass used this journal to publicize the antislavery cause and to promote the works of black writers such as Phillis Wheatley, a poet who lived at the time of the American Revolution.

Some abolitionists grew so disillusioned with the United States that they simply left the country. Reverend Alexander Crummell and Edward Wilmot Blyden founded a colony of freed American blacks in Liberia, a country on the coast of West Africa. Martin R. Delany, a black physician, led an effort to establish a colony in Africa at the bend of the Niger River. He returned to the United States in 1865 and led black troops who fought in the Union army. Like other abolitionists, he threw himself wholeheartedly into the violent struggle over slavery between Northern and Southern states, a bloody conflict that would claim the lives of more than 500,000 soldiers and countless civilians, known to history as the Civil War. ✀

The masthead of the August 3, 1831, edition of The Liberator.

The Shores family poses in front of their house in Custer County, Nebraska, in 1887.

THE CIVIL WAR AND RECONSTRUCTION

The Civil War claimed more lives than any other armed conflict in American history. This four-year contest between the Northern Union and the Southern Confederacy—lasting from 1861 to 1865—was sparked by bitter controversy about the future of slavery in the United States. Much of the strife centered around the South's desire to extend slavery into newly acquired U.S. territories and the North's determination to confine it to the Southern states.

The Missouri Compromise

In 1803 the United States had completed the Louisiana Purchase, a transaction that doubled the nation's land mass. Under this agreement, the United States acquired from France territory in what are today the states of Arkansas, Kansas, Louisiana, Nebraska, Oklahoma, South Dakota, Iowa, Minnesota, South Dakota, and Missouri.

In 1820 a crisis arose concerning the expansion of slavery into the land gained through the Louisiana Purchase. The new territory of Missouri stood to the north of the Mason-Dixon Line, the traditional boundary between free and slaveholding states, but many of the Southern whites who claimed settlements in Missouri had brought their slaves with them.

Then Missouri applied for statehood. The House of Representatives approved a bill admitting it to the Union but with an amendment that prohibited the entrance of additional slaves into the state. Northerners in the Senate, however, prevented the bill's passage, claiming that the admission to the Union of a new slaveholding state would upset the balance of power between the 11 free states of the North and the 11 slaveholding states of the South.

Debates raged in the Senate. Each side advanced its cause with such fervor that it seemed enmity about the expansion of slavery might hopelessly poison relations between the two regions. "This momentous question, like a fire bell in the night, awakened and filled me with terror," wrote Thomas Jefferson. John Quincy Adams echoed this sentiment in his diary: "I take it for granted that the present question is a mere preamble—a title-page to a great, tragic volume."

In January 1820, Congress averted a schism by passing a series of measures known collectively as the Missouri Compromise. The Senate voted to admit Missouri as a slave state and to counterbalance this act by speeding the admission of Maine into the Union as a free state. The compromise also extended the boundary between slave and free states to territory west of the Mississippi River, using the southern border of Missouri, near the 36th parallel, as the northernmost point where slavery could be practiced. Henceforth, Missouri was to be the only slave state above this line.

From 1820 until the outbreak of the Civil War in 1861 violent debates about the future of slavery factionalized Congress.

THE AFRO-AMERICANS

This agreement stemmed the conflict until the 1840s, when the cultivation of cotton spread into what is now Texas, an area that at the time belonged to Mexico. In 1845, Congress annexed Texas, and war broke out with Mexico. The United States won in 1848, and the expansion-minded country controlled not only Texas, but also the territory that would become Arizona, California, New Mexico, and Utah.

Bloodshed in Kansas

Texas's admittance to the Union in 1845 and the acquisition of new land in the West renewed debates about slavery and ushered in an era of furious sectional strife. The slave states threatened to secede from the Union if the Senate prohibited slavery in the newly gained territories, and America came perilously close to civil war. Armed battle was postponed by the resulting Compromise of 1850. Under its provisions, California joined the Union as a free state, offsetting the earlier admittance of Texas. Most of the remaining territory was given the right to decide the slavery issue for itself. To placate the abolitionist forces in the country, the Senate abolished the slave trade in Washington, D.C.; to appease the South, it strengthened the Fugitive Slave Law of 1793.

The fragile peace effected by the compromise lasted only until 1854 when a senior senator from Illinois, Stephen A. Douglas, reawakened the bitter enmity between North and South. A seasoned politician, Douglas favored a "continuous line of settlements [from the Atlantic] to the Pacific Ocean" and thus introduced into the Senate a bill proposing that the Great Plains be reorganized as the Territory of Nebraska. This vast acreage lay north of the 36th parallel, the boundary of slave states as set forth in the Missouri Compromise. Its designation as a territory—the first step to achieving statehood—would eventually tip the balance of power toward the free states of the North.

Douglas knew he faced opposition from his Southern colleagues in the Senate. He won their support by

The Swan Swamp Massacre in 1858, one of many vicious confrontations between abolitionists and pro-slavery forces that earned Kansas the sobriquet "Bleeding Kansas."

incorporating a proposal for an outright repeal of the Missouri Compromise into his Nebraska bill: Each U.S. territory and state—even those north of the 36th parallel—would adopt the policy of popular sovereignty, deciding for itself by vote whether to nullify or legalize slavery. Douglas's proposal outraged Northern politicians. For three months they tried unsuccessfully to defeat this measure, which nonetheless was passed by Congress in 1854. The Great Plains gained official status as not one, but two territories: Kansas and Nebraska.

In 1855, Kansas became the battleground of abolitionist and pro-slavery forces when slaveholding residents of neighboring Missouri tried to influence the elections that would ultimately legalize or outlaw slavery in Kansas. Partisans on both sides engaged in armed warfare. So many people lost their lives that the observers dubbed the territory "Bleeding Kansas." The abolitionists won the struggle after much loss of life, and a slave-free Kansas finally achieved statehood in 1861.

Dred Scott and John Brown

In 1857 the growing abolitionist movement suffered a setback when the United States Supreme Court handed down a controversial decision in the case of *Dred Scott V. Sandford*. Dred Scott, a black slave, had been taken by his Missouri master to the free-soil state of Illinois, from which both later returned to Missouri. Back home again, he brought suit against his owner on the grounds that he had legally become emancipated by living within a free-soil state.

The Supreme Court ruled against Scott, declaring that as a black man he was not a United States citizen and thus had no right to bring a suit in a federal court. More important, the Court ruled that a slave did not automatically gain his liberty by entering a free state. Under this logic, a man who resided in free territory could nevertheless own slaves. He had only to travel into a slave state, buy as many slaves as he desired, and take them home, where they would remain slaves ever after. After the *Dred Scott* ruling no former slave could find a safe haven within the United States. This decision made it increasingly obvious to abolitionists that slavery would never be ended without a full-scale war.

Two years after the *Dred Scott* case, an abolitionist named John Brown—a veteran of Bloody Kansas—organized a plot to free Southern slaves through armed intervention. In order to secure sufficient weaponry, he led a raiding party of 13 whites and 5 blacks into the federal arsenal at Harpers Ferry, Virginia. Brown wrested control of the armory, killed the town's mayor, and seized several hostages before he was he was captured by federal authorities and hanged two months later on December 2, 1859.

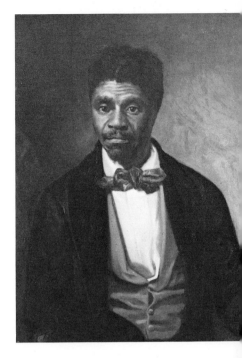

An oil portrait of Dred Scott painted by 19th-century artist Louis Schultze.

The Republican Party

In 1854, a new political party, known as the Republican party, was formed. It was a coalition that included not a single member from a Southern state. In 1860, an election year, the Republican party adopted a plank in its presidential platform opposing further expansion of slavery. The nominee of the party that year was Abraham Lincoln, a former congressman from Illinois and a Republican since 1856.

Lincoln considered slavery a moral evil, but he himself was not an abolitionist. He favored not an abrupt ending to slavery, but a gradual liberation of blacks

Abraham Lincoln sat for this studio portrait on August 13, 1860, when he was the Republican nominee for the presidency.

from bondage, to be completed by the year 1900. Lincoln also believed that slave owners should be compensated for the loss of their property and that freed blacks should establish colonies somewhere outside the United States, perhaps in Africa or the Caribbean. Lincoln won support throughout the North for his stand against the expansion of slavery. In 1860 he was elected 16th president of the United States.

Lincoln's victory threw the South into revolt. By the day of his inauguration in March 1861, seven states—Alabama, Florida, Georgia, Louisiana, Mississippi, South Carolina, and Texas—had seceded from the Union to form a coalition they called the Confederacy. One month later, on April 12, Confederate gunfire sounded over Fort Sumter, a federal stronghold located off the coast of South Carolina. Lincoln responded to this attack by issuing a call for 75,000 volunteers to man the Union army. His rallying of military troops forced states in the upper South to proclaim their loyalty for one of the two sides, and Arkansas, North Carolina, Virginia, and Tennessee joined the Confederacy. Lincoln later summed up his reasons for embarking on war in a single sentence: "My paramount object in this struggle is to save the Union, and is not either to save or to destroy slavery."

Once the war began, abolitionists presented the president with two ultimatums: They called for the emancipation of the slaves and for the right of freed blacks to fight with the Union against slavery. Eventually, Lincoln acceded to both demands. Nearly 185,000 blacks fought valiantly during the Civil War and about 38,000 of them gave their lives to the Union cause. Sixteen blacks received Congressional Medals of Honor for bravery in action. Despite countless acts of heroism on the part of black soldiers, fewer than 100 were promoted to officer. Black troops, which were segregated from white Union forces, usually fought under white officers and received lower pay than white soldiers. Until 1864, every black enlisted received only $7 a month, whereas their white counterparts earned $13 or more. Black soldiers faced other forms of discrimination as well. Several white officers, such as Union general William Tecumseh Sherman, refused to command them at all. To their credit, black enlisted men fought with a tenacity that impressed their white officers.

On September 23, 1862, Lincoln satisfied the first of the abolitionists' demands when he issued the Emancipation Proclamation, a document that freed the slaves in all states still in rebellion as of January 1, 1863. Lincoln explained the logic behind his proclamation in an interview with the New York *Tribune* in 1862: "If I could save the Union without freeing any slave, I would do it; and if I could save it by freeing all the slaves I would do it; and if I could save it by freeing some and leaving others alone, I would also do that."

Ultimately, Lincoln chose this last course of action. The Emancipation Proclamation bolstered the Union's efforts, but it produced no instant victory for the North. The War Between the States—as it was called by the Confederacy—dragged on until April 1865, the historic day that Confederate general Robert E. Lee surrendered to Union general Ulysses Grant in Appomattox, Virginia.

The end of the Civil War brought freedom to nearly 4 million slaves and a great sense of optimism to blacks throughout the United States. During the days immediately after the North proclaimed victory, liberated slaves were filled with jubilation. Freedmen, as both males and females were called, celebrated on plantations or at crossroads between them. In December 1865, Congress passed the 13th Amendment to the Constitution of the United States, guaranteeing the hard-won freedom of black slaves: "Neither slavery nor involuntary servitude . . . shall exist within the United States."

After Appomattox

The end of the Civil War destroyed the institution of slavery in the South, but it did not vanquish the racism of white Southerners, who wanted their former slaves to retain their inferior status. Confederates showed little remorse for having enslaved the blacks. In fact, they

The 107th U.S. Colored Infantry Guard of the Union army stand in front of their guardhouse.

insisted the South be readmitted to the Union without further delay or punishment from the North. Southerners argued that the Union had already exacted a terrible retribution in their territory: Nearly 250,000 men had been lost (and thousands more incapacitated), and the region's economy was shattered from the wreckage of Southern cities, small farms, and plantations.

But the Northerners were not satisfied with just the military defeat of the South. They wanted to effect permanent political and social change there and to ensure that slavery would never rear its ugly head again. In particular, a core of Republican politicians insisted that the Southern states recognize the civil rights of blacks and that legislatures below the old Mason-Dixon line redistribute privately held land. Thus, they hoped, political control in the South would be wrested from an elite group of planters, who might well mount another drive to secede.

Presidential Reconstruction

Activities in the South during the era of Presidential Reconstruction—as the years 1865–67 were later known—aroused considerable apprehension on the part of Northerners. Southern legislatures contained many former Confederate army officers and politicians. They voted to renounce secession and to ratify the 13th Amendment, but in truth they wanted to keep blacks in a position of subservience.

Claiming they, better than Northerners, truly understood "their" blacks, whites passed a series of laws, known as *Black Codes*, meant to curtail the activities of freedmen. The codes varied from state to state, but all of them forbade freedmen from carrying firearms; set restrictions on jobs freedmen could hold; and limited the amount of property they could acquire.

The worst aspect of the Black Codes was the vagrancy laws, which provided that any unemployed or idle freedman could be arrested and arbitrarily placed in a job. Although the war left thousands unemployed among both whites and blacks, the former were allowed to go free, but the latter now found themselves "assigned" to work on the plantations where they had once been slaves. The vagrancy laws enabled courts of law to order freed blacks back onto plantations. They also provided for the forced apprenticeship of black children to the former white masters of their parents. It was a strange kind of freedom for blacks.

The Republican-controlled legislature was appalled by the Black Codes and refused to seat new Southern congressmen and senators when Congress convened in late 1865. Aroused by Southern intransigence, the Republican legislators passed a series of laws (many of them over presidential vetoes) that overturned the first phase of Reconstruction and instituted a new program of change, called *Radical Reconstruction*, within the South. As a part of this revolutionary program, Congress extended the right to vote to all freedmen, thus granting formerly unheard of power to blacks while also enabling Republicans to win a constituency in the South for the first time.

In 1867 Congress divided the South into five military districts, each operating under the authority of a presidentially appointed army general, and also disenfranchised most Confederate army officers and politicians. The acts encouraged a new political order by providing for state constitutional conventions to meet with delegates elected by members of both races. For the first time, blacks were to have the right to participate in the governing process.

The South complied with the dictates of the Reconstruction Acts only because the military now occupied their territory, enforcing the new laws. By 1868 each state had held a constitutional convention, attended by black delegates, in which universal manhood suffrage was adopted, the black codes abolished, and a public school system set up for children of all races. The 14th Amendment and the civil rights acts of 1866 and 1875 gave freedmen additional liberty by granting them access to public places on an unrestricted basis.

In this 1872 cartoon General Ulysses S. Grant sits atop a carpetbag, symbol of the "carpetbaggers" who dominated Southern politics during Reconstruction.

Afro-Americans

Emancipation throughout the South was followed by a period of intense confusion in which blacks made the dramatic transition from slavery to citizenship. Afro-Americans tested their unfamiliar freedom by leaving the plantations and migrating to new areas, refusing to work for overseers, and voting and holding office. They were aided in their efforts by the Freedmen's Bureau, an organization created and funded by the Congress. The bureau performed acts of public service such as enrolling black children in schools, representing blacks in courts of law, and supervising their labor agreements with white companies. Most important, the Freedmen's Bureau provided a refuge for blacks, a place where they could usually find sympathy, help, and protection.

The bureau encouraged blacks to remain on the plantation and to work in agriculture. This would give blacks a means of economic support and also help counter the chaos disrupting Southern society. Most blacks followed this advice and remained on the plantation as sharecroppers, farmers who rented their land not with money but with a portion of their yearly crop. The arrangement was agreed upon with a bank or a private landowner. Sharecropping proved instrumental to restoring the Southern economy. By 1866 most freedmen were living and working on farms and plantations, for themselves or for wages. Very few blacks possessed the means to purchase their own land outright.

Major changes had altered the lives of the freedmen. Slavery was only a few years dead and most blacks were still poor, uneducated, and ruled by white society, yet their lives were vastly improved compared to the degradation of slavery. They could no longer be bought and sold or forcibly separated from their families. They could no longer be physically punished without a trial. They received wages for their labor. A new black community was growing out of the ashes of slavery. Blacks developed new independence and sought to separate themselves from their former oppressors as much as was possible.

The central institution in the black community became the church. Blacks in the South broke away from white Christian sects, such as the Baptists and Methodists, and set up their own churches as soon as possible. And black ministers—along with politicians, educators, and other professionals—stood at the top of black society.

Blacks in Southern Politics

During Reconstruction, the most important government positions were held by scalawags, white southern Republicans, and carpetbaggers, northerners who came south during this era. Contrary to popular perceptions, black officials did not form a majority in the South. With the exception of the lower house of the South Carolina legislature, where for a time blacks held a majority of the seats, the proportion of black officeholders fell below their percentage of the population. Fourteen black men served in the House of Representatives between 1869 and 1877. And two black Mississippians— Blanche K. Bruce, a former slave, and Hiram Revels— served in the House of Representatives between 1869 and 1877. No black ever achieved the rank of governor, although the black lieutenant governor of Louisiana, P. B. S. Pinchback, served as acting governor for more than a month.

Black politicians contributed greatly to the Reconstruction effort: They led the way in establishing the South's first public school system and they expanded and modernized the public transportation system. But these improvements created new dilemmas for the South. In order to pay for schools, bridges, roads, and railroads, many Reconstruction legislatures levied a new set of duties and those who did not incurred a considerable debt for their state.

Blanche K. Bruce was elected U.S. senator from Mississippi in 1874.

Ku Klux Klansmen, recognizable by their white hoods, were largely responsible for the racial violence that for much of the 20th century kept Southern blacks in a state of terror.

States suffered from not only increased taxes but also widespread corruption within their governments. Republican politicians—the vast majority of them white—participated in graft, jobbery, and bribe taking. They padded expense accounts and skimmed funds from public appropriations. The 1860s and 1870s were a time of widespread corruption throughout the nation, not just in the South. Indeed, the moral laxness of southerners occurred on a small scale, and blacks acted much less fraudulently than their white counterparts. But white opponents of Radical Reconstruction accused blacks of being at the forefront of the corruption and turned public opinion against the Republican governments. When their enemies combined the corruption issue with appeals to white solidarity, blacks found themselves winning fewer and fewer elections.

Whites seized upon the opportunity to rob blacks of their political gains. They first used fraudulent practices to reduce the number of black ballots. When that tactic failed, they began a campaign of terror designed to drive blacks from office and the polls. Organizations such as the Ku Klux Klan—a secret society established by ex-Confederates in 1866—lynched, murdered, beat, harassed, and threatened black voters. Although often outnumbered and unarmed, blacks fought back in pitched battles that raged through Memphis, Tennessee, in 1866; Meridian, Mississippi, in 1871; and Hamburg and Charleston, South Carolina, in 1876.

These events drove black and white politicians out of the Republican party. Conservative white southerners—all of them Democrats—gradually returned to power and "redeemed" their home territory from Republican and black rule. Some states, such as Tennessee and Virginia, were "redeemed" as early as 1869 and 1870, respectively. Democrats presented themselves as the white man's party and branded all those who refused to support or cooperate with them as traitors to their race and to the South.

By the mid-1870s, Republicans outside of the South were beginning to see blacks as a liability, and a majority of the party had begun to believe that their grand experiment of social transformation in the South had failed. Black Republicans became increasingly isolated, and the party factionalized into a black wing, called the *black and tans*, and a white wing, known as the *lily-whites*. In order to salvage their political careers many white politicians bolted for the Democratic party.

By 1877 the Radical Republicans had lost control of the South. They agreed to end Reconstruction, withdraw federal troops, and let the South solve its own racial problems. The great experiment had ended. Whites then embarked on a 20-year campaign of racial disenfranchisement and discrimination that forced blacks into second-class citizenship. White supremacy came to dominate every area of southern life. According to historian Carl Degler:

> The inability of the radicals to translate their
> egalitarian ideals into reality through the use of force
> brought an end to the first phase of the search for a
> place for the black man in America. During the years
> which followed, the South was left free to work out for
> itself what it considered the Negro's proper niche.
> Contrary to popular conceptions of Reconstruction and
> its aftermath, the South was neither united nor decided
> on what that position should be. The evolution of the
> region's place for the Negro would take another
> generation. ❧

Mr. and Mrs. Emmet J. Scott pose with their children in about 1900.

JIM CROW AND SEGREGATION

After Reconstruction and the withdrawal of federal troops from the South, blacks found themselves at the mercy of a hostile white population that subjected them to discrimination, mob violence, and, worst of all, political disenfranchisement. Blacks continued to vote and hold office until late in the 1890s, in some cases risking their personal safety to do so. But by the turn of the century they had lost virtually all their political power. The last black congressman from the South left Congress in 1901. Not until 1967 did another black man from the South, Andrew Young of Georgia, win election to the House of Representatives. Some conservative blacks even voted for the Democratic ticket in order to be allowed a small voice in party politics.

As the number of successful Democratic candidates increased, the whites who supported them grew bolder in their tactics, often resorting to illegal measures to ensure Democratic victories: They stuffed ballot boxes, threw out black votes during the counting process, and issued false election returns. Finally, whites passed a series of discriminatory voting laws that effectively silenced blacks. In time, prejudicial laws would extend into other realms, namely schools and public transportation. As a body, this legislation was known as Jim Crow laws, named after the buffoonish central character of a racist 19th-century song-and-dance act that mocked blacks.

Because the Constitution prohibited racially based discrimination, Jim Crow laws avoided specific mention of race and did not openly prohibit blacks from voting. The only Jim Crow voting law that specifically mentioned race was the white primary ban, which forbade blacks from voting in Democratic primaries. Otherwise, the laws consisted of requirements that seemed to have no racial purpose, though they strategically worked against blacks. For example, under Jim Crow laws all voters had to pay a two-dollar poll tax when they registered to vote. Most black voters, and many whites as well, were simply too poor to afford the tax and thus were deemed ineligible to cast their ballot.

(continued on page 73)

An etching from Frank Leslie's Illustrated Newspaper *depicts South Carolina blacks traveling to the polls. After "redemption" Southern legislatures disenfranchised the majority of black citizens.*

A PANORAMA OF THE PERFORMING ARTS

(Overleaf) *The Alvin Ailey American Dance Theater*
performs Revelations, *a ballet choreographed to a selection*
of spirituals.

Black dance ranges from the glamour of Broadway, epitomized by tap and jazz veteran Maurice Hines (left), to the classical elegance of the Dance Theater of Harlem's Swan Lake, to the urban vitality of break dancing (above).

Black excellence in two musical forms, opera and blues, is personified in baritone Simon Estes and singer B. B. King: (clockwise from left) King accompanies himself on his guitar, "Lucille"; Estes takes center stage in Porgy and Bess; *he plays opposite diva Leontyne Price in Verdi's masterpiece* Aida.

Rock 'n' roller Chuck Berry jams at his 60th-birthday concert, backed up by Rolling Stone member Keith Richards (opposite); Louis Armstrong improvises a horn solo (above); and bandleader Cab Calloway rehearses for a Washington gala.

The Fat Boys have helped popularize rap songs, in which performers rhythmically speak lyrics that often carry a social or political message.

(continued from page 64)

In addition to the tax, legislators instituted "literacy and understanding" tests in which the voter had to prove his ability to read and understand a specific document, usually the state or federal constitution or the Declaration of Independence, in order to register. Later many states added the requirement that voters hold a certain value of land or property. Generally, known as the Mississippi Plan (for the state that first implemented them), these laws kept tens of thousands of black adults off the voting lists.

One problem created by the Jim Crow laws was that they also disenfranchised thousands of poor white voters. Thus many states adopted a "Grandfather Clause," which enabled a voter to forgo the poll tax if his ancestor had voted in 1860—when blacks were still slaves. The Supreme Court declared the grandfather clauses unconstitutional in *Guinn v. U.S.* in 1915.

In cities, where better educated, middle-class blacks could circumvent the discriminatory laws, whites resorted to race riots to drive black politicians from office and in some cases from the city as well. In 1898, whites in Wilmington, North Carolina, staged an effective coup d'état that drove both black members of the city council and the black sheriff from office amid much bloodshed. In Atlanta, Georgia, a white-instigated race riot in 1906 culminated in pitched street battles that discouraged blacks from political participation.

White supremacy became so nearly complete that even well-to-do blacks finally gave up hope and acceded to the inevitable. In 1877, the South Carolina legislature had 39 black members in its lower house. By 1890 the number had shrunk to 6, and by 1900 there were none. Mississippi followed a similar course, as did other Southern states. The Democratic party, the bastion of an elite planter class and of former Confederate officers, was winning 96 percent of all elections. The South's 9 million blacks, numbering just more than 11 percent of the nation's entire population, had disappeared from the public arena.

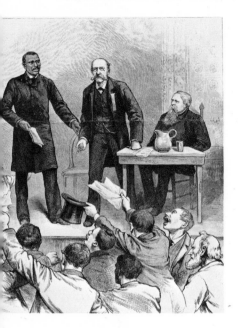

A black delegate speaks at the 10th annual convention of the Knights of Labor. During the late 19th century blacks maintained some of their political power by forming alliances with white organizations and political parties.

Fusion Politics

In order to resist annihilation, black politicians of the 1880s resorted to an old trick and allied—or fused—themselves and their constituents with political parties willing to be of some service to the black community. In return, black leaders instructed their followers to vote for the candidates of that party.

The most successful fusion was born of an alliance between poor black and white farmers, who composed the membership of three agrarian parties: the Northern Farmers Alliance, the Southern Farmers Alliance, and the Colored Farmers Alliance. In the 1880s, these groups formed a National Farmers Alliance, a forerunner of the Populist movement of the 1890s. The marriage between Republicans and Populists worked well for a time, but the conservative Democrats, who were losing seats to fusion candidates, responded with a massive wave of disenfranchising legislation that hurt Populists as well as blacks. Gradually, the Populist party turned against blacks, unleashing the racist tirades of Tom Watson and other former supporters of the black community. In the late 1890s, whites solidified behind color lines and thereafter race became a primary consideration in regional and national politics.

Segregation in Education

Throughout the South, the races became polarized not just in the realm of politics but in all areas. States passed laws that legalized the preexisting custom of keeping blacks and whites apart, or segregated. This system advocated a policy of maintaining "separate but equal" schools, transportation, and housing for the races; in truth, whites alone benefited from the system. It increased their domination of the South politically, economically, and socially.

The first segregation laws affected public schools. Since they were founded—after the Civil War—these had never mixed black and white students. During Reconstruction, the Freedmen's Bureau actually supported such schools, on the assumption that special institutions for blacks would include a curriculum developed expressly to suit them. But over the years black schools got the short end from state legislatures, which skimped on equipment, building maintenance, and teachers' salaries. After 1900, schools for white pupils received twice as many funds as those for blacks.

Similar injustices also occurred at the university level. Black colleges, which depended on financial contributions from Northern white philanthropists, had trouble obtaining support unless their curriculums emphasized manual and vocational training. The issue of higher education split the black community. Liberals maintained that students deserved a chance to develop their intellect and creativity. Conservatives argued that training students as skilled craftsmen was better than not training them at all—an argument also advanced by many racist whites. In the end, black education proved "separate" but not "equal."

Students gather in front of a "Negro school" in about 1900.

The Spread of Jim Crow

In time, Jim Crow laws applied to public transportation. Many Southern cities started separating whites from blacks in streetcars, and states quickly followed by keeping them apart in railroad cars. In 1881, the Tennessee legislature became the first in the country to require "colored" travelers to sit in Jim Crow cars, which were nothing more than the smoking cars. Throughout the South, wealthy black travelers who for years had purchased a first-class ticket and sat in the first-class coach found themselves forced to tolerate uncomfortable bench seats.

In 1887, W. H. Council, the president of an all-black college in Alabama, suffered just such an indignity when, in spite of his first-class ticket, the conductor forced him to move to the Jim Crow car. He filed a complaint with the Interstate Commerce Commission, which responded with a ruling that permitted separate facilities on public transportation so long as they were equivalent to white ones. Black Americans were outraged at this decision. They well knew that the separate

A black passenger is expelled from a Philadelphia railway car in this etching from the Illustrated London News *in 1856.*

facilities were not equal and were not intended to be.

In 1896, Jim Crow was again challenged in the historic case *Plessy v. Ferguson*. Homer Plessy, a black man from New Orleans, was arrested for refusing to move from the whites-only coach on the East Louisiana Railroad line. He challenged his conviction on the grounds that it violated his rights under the 14th Amendment. The case eventually found its way to the Supreme Court, which in its ruling deemed separate facilities for blacks constitutionally valid if they were equal to those reserved for white people. Justice John Marshall Harlan, the lone dissenter in the case, declared the decision as harmful to the country as that in the *Dred Scott* case. He further added that, "Our Constitution is color-blind and neither knows nor tolerates classes among citizens. In respect of civil rights, all citizens are equal before the law."

The landmark decision in *Plessy v. Ferguson* opened the door to a new wave of segregation laws. Southern states segregated waiting rooms, lavatories, water fountains, lunch counters, prisons, poorhouses, public parks, restaurants, even cemeteries and factories. Southern cities adopted segregated housing ordinances and went so far as to use a Jim Crow Bible in courtrooms. Piece by piece the bricks were cemented into the wall of segregation, and blacks were forced to tolerate second-class citizenship.

As historian C. Vann Woodward has pointed out, segregation was by no means uniform throughout the South. In some areas the black middle class grew and prospered free from daily harassment and humiliation. In other areas, whites ignored Jim Crow laws and allowed or even encouraged black voting. Blacks continued to hold local offices, such as sheriff and justice of the peace, and sat on city councils until 1900. And in many southern cities, blacks challenged Jim Crow by boycotting segregated streetcar lines and stores. Still, the rule of the day was segregation. And to black people living in the South it seemed that the occasional victory was followed by more setbacks. Afro-Americans in the North, too, suffered racial prejudice, but the North never approached the South in the viciousness and pervasiveness of its discrimination.

Mob Rule

Worse even than segregation was the racial violence that terrorized blacks during the 1890s. During this period, a wave of lynchings, unprecedented in their frequency, swept through the rural South. Some occurred in cities, but most took place in isolated rural areas where blacks composed between 40 and 50 percent of the population and thus were perceived by hostile whites as a potential threat to white domination.

During a lynching, mob members openly flaunted their identity before hundreds or even thousands of onlookers. People from all levels of society attended lynch-

An Indiana mob attends a lynching in 1930. The practice of lynching was not limited to the South and was responsible for thousands of deaths.

ing bees, as they were called. Men, women, and children dressed in their Sunday best for this special event and looked on in fascination as the victim, often a young black man falsely accused of murder or arson, was hanged. During the 1890s, this scene was repeated more than 1,400 times. Sometimes the victim was a black politician who had refused to resign in favor of a white man. Southern whites claimed the chief cause of lynching was interracial rape, but the statistics did not support their contention. In fact, less than 20 percent of all lynchings involved a charge of rape or sexual assault against a white woman. The lynch mob acted with virtual impunity; less than one percent of their participants were ever arrested and indicted, let alone tried and convicted.

The lynch mob became the most feared symbol of white supremacy in the South, upholding the sentiment of Jim Crow. In the few areas where segregation laws did not extend, a single lynching might discourage black voting for years. How could the South so freely discriminate against and terrorize Afro-Americans? For a combination of reasons: Republicans had all but deserted the cause of racial equality, and northerners withdrew their support of southern blacks by ignoring their plight, even denying civil rights to blacks who had moved northward. Thus, blacks found themselves isolated, and oppressed. The white South had achieved what it once had under slavery—the creation of a work force it could control.

Booker T. Washington at the Tuskegee Institute in 1906.

The Black Response to White Supremacy

During this bleak era in their history, black Americans had little to comfort them: neither relief from daily toil nor certainty that their lot would someday improve. But they did find hope in a succession of black leaders who devoted their own lives to bettering those of American blacks. The first to rise to prominence was Booker T. Washington, an Afro-American born into slavery in 1856. Washington headed the Tuskegee Institute—an

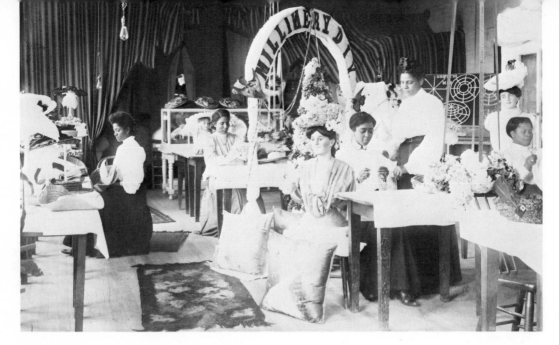

Black women students learn millinery at the Tuskegee Institute in 1906.

industrial school located in Tuskegee, Alabama—and advocated vocational education for blacks, saying that they must learn a trade in order to earn economic independence and self-respect. During his tenure at Tuskegee, Washington made the acquaintance of George Washington Carver, who served as the school's director of agricultural research and achieved his own fame for scientific work. He discovered hundreds of uses for the sweet potato, the peanut, and the soybean—crops he believed would revolutionize southern agriculture.

Through his "Tuskegee machine" Booker T. Washington became a leader as well as an educator. In 1895 he stirred controversy within the black community and attracted international attention by telling a predominantly white crowd at the Cotton States Exposition in Atlanta, Georgia, that blacks would temporarily accept disenfranchisement and the loss of political power and accept segregation. "In all things that are purely social," he said, "we can be as separate as the fingers, yet one as the hand in all things essential to mutual progress."

Washington faced fierce opposition from other blacks, including a Harvard-educated intellectual named William Edward Burghardt (W. E. B.) Du Bois.

Du Bois was born in Great Barrington, Massachusetts, in 1868, and in 1895 he became Harvard's first black Ph.D. In 1903 Du Bois published a scathing essay entitled "Of Mr. Booker T. Washington and Others" in his book *Souls of Black Folk*, denouncing Washington's willingness to accept a "temporary" second-class citizenship for Afro-Americans. Du Bois demanded immediate restoration of political rights for blacks and advocated a "Talented Tenth" to act as racial leaders. He also encouraged blacks to embrace their African heritage. In 1909, Du Bois joined with leading white reformers to create the National Association for the Advancement of Colored People (NAACP), an organization pledged to the elimination of segregation and other forms of discrimination.

Du Bois's views proved as controversial as Washington's, and before long they, too, caused spirited debate within the black community. His chief adversary was William Monroe Trotter, born in 1872 in Hyde Park, New York. Trotter earned an undergraduate degree from Harvard, then made his reputation as editor

W. E. B. Du Bois sits in his office at the Crisis, *a magazine published by the NAACP.*

William Monroe Trotter helped found the Niagara movement— a forerunner of the NAACP— along with W. E. B. Du Bois.

of the *Guardian*, a newspaper he founded in Boston, Massachusetts, in 1901. From its pages Trotter argued that if blacks tolerated adversity (as Washington had advised) or overemphasized their African heritage (as Du Bois thought they should), they would only impede the process of their integration and assimilation into American society. His advocacy of immediate integration foreshadowed the civil rights movement of the 1960s.

The Emigration Movement

While Washington, Du Bois, and Trotter fought against the late 19th-century oppression of blacks, another black leader, Bishop Henry McNeal Turner, became the spokesman for Afro-Americans who decided their best hope for a decent life lay in a return to Africa. Born to freedmen in South Carolina in 1834, Turner grew to adulthood with a keen awareness of his family's low social status. Of America, Turner said, "We were born here, raised here, fought, bled and died here, and have a thousand times more right here than hundreds of thousands of those who help to snub, proscribe and persecute us, and that is one of the reasons I almost despise the land of my birth." His message held a special appeal for poor southern blacks, who had despaired of hoping that life in the United States held any promise for them.

In the early 1890s, Turner joined forces with the American Colonization Society (ACS). This group had already sponsored the migration of approximately 100 black Americans to Liberia annually. Turner and the ACS helped smooth the way for additional emigrants. In 1891 Turner himself visited his ancestral homeland and wrote glowingly of its opportunities, all but ignoring the widespread poverty and disease in western Africa. His accounts of life across the ocean captured the imagination of blacks back home, and by 1892 thousands had begun to apply for passage aboard the small ships leaving New York for Liberia. Strapped by a lack of funds, the ACS was forced to turn all of them away and as a consequence collapsed entirely.

Migration North

For the great majority of black people living in the South, a less distant journey seemed a sure means of obtaining relief from their daily oppression. At the beginning of the 20th century, they turned their gaze not toward Africa but toward the industrial cities of the North, whose factories offered better wages than the fields of the South.

Some blacks—and whites—had moved as early as the 1860s, but the exodus did not gather force until the 1900s. In 1910, three-fourths of the nearly 10 million Afro-Americans lived in rural areas and nine-tenths lived in the South. By 1950, three-fourths of the black population—which totaled more than 15 million—dwelled in cities and slightly more than half lived outside the South. This exodus—called the "Great Migration"—was the most significant population shift in American history and brought about a profound change in the texture of black life. ∾

In 1863 President Lincoln appointed Bishop Henry McNeal Turner chaplain to the Union army's First Regiment of Colored Troops.

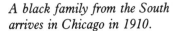

A black family from the South arrives in Chicago in 1910.

LIFE IN THE GHETTO

The Great Migration was a major turning point in the Afro-American experience. A huge portion of the black population no longer resided in the rural South but in urban centers in the North. Most black migrants took on unskilled jobs in industry—laborious and often dangerous work—that offered them higher wages than they had ever before received.

Soon reports detailing the wonderful opportunities available in Chicago, Detroit, New York City, Philadelphia, and St. Louis filtered into the South, stimulating further waves of migration. But at the close of World War I, the Northern wellspring suddenly went dry. European nations reduced their demand for U.S. goods, decreasing the production rates of American factories. The nation's economy sagged, and the number of available jobs declined. Blacks found themselves vying for employment against white veterans of the Great War—a competition that kindled resentment within both groups.

The Urban Ghetto

New arrivals from the South faced a similar struggle in their quest for decent housing. In New York City, for example, blacks who arrived at the outset of the Great Migration had lived along the northern edge of Manhattan in a neighborhood called Harlem. Once a wealthy white quarter, Harlem began accepting black

Blacks and whites work together in this New York cigar factory in about 1915.

residents in 1903, and by 1910 was home to about 5,000 black families, all squeezed into a 6-block section of the neighborhood.

In an effort to prevent the influx of more blacks, worried white residents organized the Harlem Property Owners Association. It failed to keep out blacks, and "white flight" began in earnest. Unscrupulous real estate agents capitalized on whites' fears through a practice called blockbusting. The realtors sneaked a black family onto a previously white block, thereby panicking the whites, who sold their property cheaply to the real estate company. Once the block had been busted, real estate developers renovated the housing, dividing space meant for a single family into rooms for five times as many, usually with a common kitchen. This opened up more apartments for a while, but there was not enough room for the steady stream of blacks. By the 1930s, 233 black people crowded into every square block of Harlem, whereas white Manhattanites lived with the more comfortable ratio of 133 people per square block.

Black neighborhoods across the country suffered a similar fate and rapidly deteriorated into dangerous and dirty ghettos. To make matters worse, these districts' longtime black residents often blamed their ruin on the newcomers and developed a revulsion against their brethren from the rural South. Northern blacks disdained new migrants as "country bumpkins" and often refused to admit them to fraternal organizations, churches, social clubs, and other community groups that could have eased their transition into city life. Instead, the new arrivals had to fend for themselves in an alien and often hostile environment.

Disillusioned Anew

Eventually, the antagonism between established blacks and newcomers relaxed into a mutual understanding and the two groups banded together to form a unified community of urban blacks. The turning point was World War I. By war's end nearly 367,000 Afro-Americans were called into service, 50,000 of whom actually fought overseas. Veterans returned home from the fox-

Interior of a Harlem apartment in about 1910.

holes of France with a new outlook. Europeans often treated them equitably—as Americans rather than blacks—and the soldiers learned that it was possible to live in a society free from discrimination. Veterans passed this discovery on to family and friends, and—perhaps unintentionally—fortified fellow blacks for their long struggle for equality.

America was less ready than Europe to acknowledge the accomplishments of Afro-American soldiers. Historian John Hope Franklin has pointed out that black troops were the first Allied troops to push into German-controlled territory and reach the Rhine river. The Germans called them Hell Fighters. But when the Hell Fighters returned home they were hardly honored and once again they found themselves mired in racism.

The postwar era was a time of dashed hopes not only for black veterans, but for all Afro-Americans. Their dreams of a prosperous city life curdled as they

In 1919 a wounded soldier watches a parade of the 369th Infantry, an exclusively black division of the U.S. Army.

confronted the harsh realities of workplace discrimination and the urban ghetto. They found, too, that they had failed to escape the racist violence of the South, as the Ku Klux Klan took root in Northern metropolises.

In the ill-fated summer of 1919, later called the Red Summer, Afro-Americans publicly vented their anger and frustration. Twenty race riots erupted in cities across the country, spilling blood in larger urban centers, such as Chicago, and smaller towns, such as Elaine, Arkansas. Generally, police in the various cities where the riots occurred did nothing to quell them, and in some cases they actually aided white rioters or took part in the frays themselves.

These melees signaled a new militancy among blacks, who—concentrated for the first time in small, urban neighborhoods—actively engaged whites in violent confrontation, something that had been unthinkable in the rural South. Fighting in Houston, Texas, for example, marked the first time in history that a race riot took more white than black lives. The black community had finally dared to retaliate, and Afro-Americans interpreted this new boldness as a sign that they could win victories not only in the streets but also in the arenas of politics and economics.

The Reign of Garvey

During this volatile period, one man arose to capture the attention of the masses crowded into America's ghettos—Marcus Moziah Garvey. Born on the island of Jamaica in 1887, Garvey was a self-taught orator with a magnetic personality. As a young man, he read widely, especially in the works of Booker T. Washington, and found inspiration in Washington's theories about the importance of self-help and racial solidarity for blacks.

Garvey developed his own philosophy about race and adopted a more radical stance than Washington's. He believed whites would always be prejudiced against people of African descent. He rejected integration and assimilation, arguing instead that the African in the United States and the Caribbean should develop "a distinct racial type of civilization of his own and . . . work out his salvation in his motherland."

In 1914, Garvey founded an organization that later served as the base for his back to Africa movement, the Universal Negro Improvement Association (UNIA). In its earliest days, the UNIA aimed not to relocate blacks but to heighten black pride and to introduce a program of educational and economic opportunity. Garvey also established the African Orthodox church, in which he preached that God was black and the devil white. When the UNIA failed to find a responsive audience in Jamaica, Garvey traveled to New York in 1916 and established the headquarters of his international organization in the rapidly growing black community of Harlem.

At first the UNIA attracted scant support in Harlem but, after the Red Summer politicized New York blacks, its membership grew. Garvey spread his views through his newspaper, the *Negro World*, and he soon stood at the head of a black nationalist movement that first blossomed through Afro-American communities in the 1840s and later in the 1890s, under the leadership of Du Bois and Turner. The UNIA's message of political liberation and African nationalism struck a chord deep within the oppressed masses in big-city ghettos. By August 1920, when the movement reached its peak, total membership in the UNIA—according to Garvey— numbered approximately 2 million in 30 chapters around the world. Also in 1920, Garvey presided over the First International Convention of the Negro Peoples of the World, attended by thousands of his supporters. In honor of the event, the UNIA staged an elaborate parade through the streets of Harlem.

Much of the district closed down as thousands lined the streets to watch the procession. Garvey rode in an open car, wearing an elegant uniform topped with a plumed hat. In his wake followed an army of UNIA groups. The African Legions and the Black Cross

Nurses marched with military precision and waved the UNIA's red, black, and green flag ("red for the blood that was shed in slavery, black for the noblest of all races, and green for the land of Africa"). As they paraded, the UNIA members sang their anthem, "Ethiopia, Thou Land of Our Fathers."

Later, the charismatic Garvey gave a speech, in which he told the crowd that he wanted to "retake every square inch of the 12,000,000 square miles of African territory belonging to us [all persons of African heritage] by right divine." His slogan, "Africa for the Africans at Home and Abroad," became a symbol of united opposition to the racism blacks in the Western Hemisphere endured and to the oppression that Africans faced from the European colonial powers dominating their homeland.

At the very moment of Garvey's triumph, his reign was about to end. In 1919, he had founded the Black Star Line of steamships to conduct trade between blacks in America and the Caribbean. When word of this endeavor reached UNIA members, they believed that he had established the steamship line to transport the faithful back to Africa. Indeed, in the 1920s, Garvey sent delegations to the black nation of Liberia in order to open the way for UNIA settlers. The Liberians were initially receptive to Garvey's emigration plan, but by 1924 Liberian president Charles D. B. King viewed the UNIA with extreme suspicion. He suspected Garvey of secretly scheming to take over the Liberian government. Faced also with the financial collapse of the Black Star Line, Garvey soon abandoned his plans for emigration.

At home, Garvey faced mounting opposition from the black elite, especially W. E. B. Du Bois, who labeled Garvey the worst enemy of the black race and called him an uneducated foreigner and a demagogue. Another influential man, labor and protest leader A. Philip Randolph, joined in the chorus of criticism and warned the black community that any government led by Garvey would be a reactionary dictatorship, not

In August 1924, Marcus Garvey rides in a parade to celebrate a meeting of the International Convention of the Negro Peoples of the World, which first convened in 1920.

Fashionable Harlemites stroll down Lenox Avenue, a main thoroughfare of the neighborhood during the 1930s.

a democracy. Black church leaders also aligned against Garvey. His African Orthodox church threatened to woo away the masses of black poor who composed their congregations.

In 1922, Robert Abbott, the editor of the Chicago newspaper the *Defender* and an adversary of Garvey's made it known that Garvey was about to sell stock in the UNIA without a license. A federal investigation began and uncovered irregularities in the UNIA's financial affairs. Garvey was indicted and convicted of mail fraud. Historians still debate the question of Garvey's guilt. Some have defended him as an honest man who too easily trusted unreliable "lieutenants" to run his complex and far-flung organizations. Others believe he knowingly defrauded his followers.

Garvey appealed his conviction but in 1925 was sent to the Atlanta Penitentiary. Two years later the U.S. government commuted his sentence and deported him to his native land, Jamaica, where Garvey carried on his work until his death in 1940.

The Harlem Renaissance

The decade dominated politically by Garvey also witnessed a flowering of black culture now known as the Harlem Renaissance. By 1920 Harlem had become the capital of the black world, a city within a city, in which 200,000 Afro-Americans lived within an area of 2 square miles. There some of the most talented artists in the United States gathered together and forever changed the face of American music, theater, and literature.

The Advent of Jazz

The 1920s was a period when, in the words of poet Langston Hughes, "Harlem was in Vogue." New Yorkers from every walk of life flocked uptown to Harlem to spend long evenings—they often stretched until dawn—in an array of night spots. Forty years before races generally mingled, white millionaires casually brushed shoulders with black factory hands. The main attraction for whites were fashionable clubs such as The Bamboo Inn, Mexico's, and Connie's Inn, where patrons could hear the sounds of jazz.

Jazz traced its roots to the American spirituals of the late 19th century and even further back, to the rhythms, melodies, and harmonies of West Africa. The earliest jazz musicians hailed from New Orleans, where in the early 1900s they played "Dixieland," an ensemble style that featured several instruments playing together at breakneck tempos. In the mid-1920s, Dixieland evolved into the "Western" or "Chicago" style. Its greatest figure was Louis Armstrong, a New Orleans native, whose trumpet solos introduced the spontaneous invention—or improvisation—that distinguished jazz from every other variety of music. Armstrong and other jazz masters, such as clarinetist Sidney Bechet and pianist Earl "Fatha" Hines, elevated jazz solos into musical statements of great sophistication and beauty.

The best jazz playing often occurred in jam sessions or in cutting contests. In these, young musicians competed with each other in order to win an opportunity to play with jazz giants. Milton "Mezz" Mezzrow, a white reedman from Chicago, often played in Harlem and described an after-hours cutting contest held at Mexico's:

> The contests generally happened in the early morning, after the musicians came uptown from their various jobs. There was always a small private club or a speakeasy that had a piano in it, and when some new musician came to town he was obliged to come up with his instrument and get off for the older musicians. . . . before the night was over all the cats were in some smoky room, really blowing up a breeze. If it was a close call . . . and people couldn't come to much decision about who was best—then somebody would sneak out and get [saxophonist] Coleman Hawkins, and when he unwrapped his horn it settled all arguments and sent the boys back to practice some more.

Blues queen Bessie Smith smiles for a publicity photo in 1925.

Instrumental music was the domain of male players, but women prevailed in the field of jazz singing, often performing blues numbers characterized by the themes of love, sex, poverty, and death. Harlem clubs were never more packed than when Bessie Smith, Empress of the Blues, belted out "Gulf Coast Blues" or "Baby Won't You Please Come Home" to a crowd that hung on her every note.

Born in about 1898 in Chattanooga, Tennessee, Smith was herself the protégée of Gertrude (Ma) Rainey, a vocalist who raised the singing of blues to an art form. Smith moved to New York in the early 1920s—after several years on the road—and enjoyed stardom both onstage and through best-selling sound recordings. One fan recalled her in performance:

> Bessie Smith was a fabulous deal to watch. She was a pretty large woman and she could sing the blues. . . . She dominated a stage. You didn't turn your head when she went on. You just watched Bessie. You didn't read any newspapers in a night club when she went on. She just upset you. When you say Bessie—that was it. She was unconscious of her surroundings. . . . If you had any church background, like people who came from the South as I did, you would recognize a similarity between what she was doing and what those preachers and evangelists from there did, and how they moved people. Bessie did the same thing on stage. She could bring about a mass hypnotism. When she was performing, you could hear a pin drop.

The Dean of Harlem Poets

As Armstrong enchanted listeners with his trumpet, and Bessie Smith captivated them with her song, poet contemporary Langston Hughes moved readers with his lyrical verse. Born in Joplin, Missouri, in 1902, Hughes spent his early youth working at a variety of odd jobs, including busboy, and traveling widely. In 1925 his work was introduced to white audiences by the American poet Vachel Lindsay, and one year later Hughes's first book of poems, *The Weary Blues*, was published to great acclaim. Hughes's poetry incorporated the rhythms of jazz and blues with the cadences of black speech. He drew upon all sides of black experience in his work—particularly the struggles of urban blacks.

Another major black author was novelist and folklorist Zora Neale Hurston. Like Hughes, she made music out of the rhythms of ordinary black speech. In the words of one critic, "In the speech of her characters, black voices . . . come alive. Her fidelity to diction, metaphor and syntax rings with an aching familiarity that is a testament to Hurston's skill and to the durability of black speech."

Born in 1901 in Eatonville, Florida, Hurston struggled all her life to celebrate and promote the rich heritage of American blacks, particularly rural blacks. Her most famous novel, *Their Eyes Were Watching God* (1938) describes the life of Janie, a headstrong woman who gives up a loveless but financially secure marriage in order to embark on a love affair and a subsequent journey of self-discovery. Hurston published five more novels as well as a folktale collection, an autobiography, and many short stories. Then she hit hard times. She suffered from a stroke and heart disease before dying in a welfare home in her home state in 1960. Hurston lay in an unmarked grave for more than a decade. Then another important black writer, Alice Walker, discovered Hurston's burial site and had a tombstone erected there. Walker also rescued Hurston's work from obscurity, using her own influence (much of it gained from her own success as a writer) to persuade publishers to reissue several of Hurston's novels. Thanks to Walker's efforts, Hurston's work has once again found a wide following, and she has emerged as one of the great American authors of her time.

According to novelist Sherley Anne Williams, the Harlem Renaissance amounts to "the first concerted outpourings of formal artistic expression among Afro-Americans." Even after the glory days of Harlem had ended, black artists continued to reap the rich tradition established by an earlier generation. Black authors, for

Langston Hughes visits New York's Public School 113 in 1943.

A native of Florida, Zora Neale Hurston journeyed north to study at Barnard College and—along with her contemporary Langston Hughes—introduced a uniquely black idiom into American literature.

example, produced important work in the 1930s and 1940s, especially the fiction of Richard Wright, author of *Black Boy* and *Native Son*. The 1950s saw the publication of *The Invisible Man*, by Wright's protégé Ralph Ellison. In 1965, a poll of critics and writers named this masterpiece the single best novel written by any American since World War II. Another major black writer, James Baldwin, excelled as a novelist, playwright, and essayist. His searing account of black experience—*The Fire Next Time*—caused a sensation when it appeared in The *New Yorker* magazine in 1963. Today, leading black writers include Walker, Toni Morrison, and John Edgar Wideman.

The New Deal

During the Harlem Renaissance, Afro-Americans forged a new identity, based on a decade of artistic and cultural achievement among blacks. This era saw the birth of what Howard University professor Alain Locke has called "The New Negro," whose confidence and energy seemed to overcome a sorrowful past. But at the close of the 1920s, the Jazz Age euphoria that had galvanized Harlem abruptly stopped.

In October 1929, stocks in the United States declined in value by an average of 40 percent. The crash of the stock market, in the words of one historian, "confronted the United States with its greatest crisis since the Civil War. Factories slashed production; construction practically ceased; millions of investors lost their savings; over 5,000 banks closed their doors in the first three years of the [economic] depression." A worldwide depression ensued that took its toll on Americans across the country. No group suffered more than the blacks.

The administration of President Herbert Hoover—whom the executive director of the NAACP, Walter White, referred to as "the man in the lily white house"—did so little to aid Afro-Americans that by 1933 between 25 and 40 percent of urban blacks depended on federal relief to avoid starvation. Many private charities sustained whites during this difficult

Eleanor Roosevelt (fourth from left) championed black rights throughout her lifetime.

period but discriminated against blacks in the distribution of food; some organizations bluntly refused to sponsor integrated soup kitchens.

Hope came with the election of Franklin D. Roosevelt to the presidency in 1933. He promised that "no citizen shall be permitted to starve" and that "in addition to providing emergency relief, the Federal Government should and must provide temporary work whenever that is possible." Shortly after taking office, Roosevelt inaugurated the New Deal, a program aimed at helping those hurt by the Great Depression. Many Americans, blacks among them, found employment through the New Deal's temporary work programs, such as the Public Works Administration, the Civilian Conservation Corps, and the Works Progress Administration. Roosevelt did not openly advocate equal rights for blacks, but he ensured that they reaped the benefits of his policies. Indeed, the New Deal marked the beginning of 20th-century federal involvement in civil rights. To that extent, apart from the short-term aid it gave during the depression, it set the stage for the next dramatic chapter of Afro-American history, the civil rights movement. ∾

In 1958 an Afro-American
family gathers to celebrate the
college graduation of one of its
members, Mrs. Bessie Minor
White (shown in cap and gown).

THE CIVIL RIGHTS
REVOLUTION

During World War II approximately 1 million black men and women served their country with distinction. Although they still faced discrimination, they gained entry into more branches of the armed forces than ever before, bolstering the ranks of fighting and tranportation units, the engineer corps, the signal corps, and many other divisions of Selective Service. In January 1945, the army initiated a bold plan to intermingle platoons of white and black troops to fight within Germany. The experiment met with great success, and blacks' accomplishments equaled those of the Hell Fighters feared by Germans during World War I.

At home, industrial plants joined the war effort by producing the weaponry needed to supply the troops. In the process, they won lucrative government supply contracts that enabled them to hire millions of workers and pay them more than ever before. The boom in the defense industry, along with Roosevelt's New Deal employment programs, lifted the American workforce out of its depression slump. But black workers did not share in this new abundance and stood no chance of employment in defense plants, which were controlled, by and large, by white-dominated unions.

The First March on Washington

In all of the United States, one man commanded the organizational expertise blacks desperately needed to gain access to the defense plants. He was A. Philip Randolph, the organizer and president of the Brotherhood of Sleeping Car Porters (an all-black union since 1937, the year it was founded). Randolph was a seasoned labor negotiator. He clearly perceived the racism that shut blacks out of defense plants and denied them many other opportunities enjoyed by white Americans.

In 1941, Randolph decided to combat the racist policies of defense plants in order to advance the cause of winning equality and justice for blacks. To that end, he spread news of a planned march on the nation's capital throughout the black community, calling for 50,000 to 100,000 blacks from across the country to travel to Washington, D.C., and protest the policies that withheld employment from them.

The mere threat of the march on Washington pressured President Franklin D. Roosevelt into negotiating with Randolph. Roosevelt feared social unrest among blacks and also knew that a mass demonstration against racism in Washington would tarnish the United States's image abroad as a champion of democracy. The president met several times with Randolph, who agreed to cancel the march if Roosevelt guaranteed the end of discrimination against blacks in the defense industry. On June 25, 1941, Roosevelt complied by issuing Executive Order 8802—a landmark document in black American history. It declared that "there shall be no discrimination in the employment of workers in defense industries or Government because of race, creed, color, or national origin." This was the first presidential directive on race relations since Reconstruction and once again aligned the federal government with the well-being of the country's black citizens.

As a result of the executive order, defense plants hired about 2 million blacks, admitting many of them into unionized jobs. The number of blacks enrolled in labor unions rose to 1.23 million, an increase of nearly

100 percent. In addition, 200,000 blacks found employment with the federal government, which began hiring Afro-Americans in greater numbers than ever before. From 1941 until the war's end in 1945, black Americans achieved significant economic gains—the first step in preparing them for the struggle to come.

As the nation entered the peaceful and prosperous 1950s, Afro-Americans grew even more determined to end racial injustice. In 1947, they saw two of their own break into America's favorite pastime, when second baseman Jackie Robinson donned the uniform of the Brooklyn Dodgers and infielder (later outfielder) Larry Doby joined the Cleveland Indians. Blacks knew, however, that such advancements, though significant, would never substitute for full integration into the American mainstream.

In 1948, Afro-Americans (only one quarter of whom qualified to vote; Jim Crow still shut them out of southern polls) supported Democratic incumbent Harry S. Truman in his victorious presidential campaign. Today, historians credit Truman's narrow margin of success to the black urban vote he received. Blacks anticipated his return to office with great happiness and hoped that his administration would help advance the cause of civil rights. Truman made some important moves (such as ending segregation in the armed forces) but he did not actively press for civil rights legislation. Black Americans realized that, in the words of A. Philip Randolph, they would have to begin exacting the justice owed them by the federal government.

In 1936 A. Philip Randolph delivers an address to the National Negro Congress, for which he served as president.

Separate but Not Equal

In the early 1950s, black leaders decided the time had come to challenge the principle of segregation. They focused their attack on the public schools of the South, which cheated black children of an opportunity to receive an education comparable to that of white students.

In 1951, Thurgood Marshall, the head of the NAACP's Legal Defense Fund, began to develop a case challenging the legality of school segregation. Local

NAACP lawyers (from left to right) George Hayes, Thurgood Marshall, and James N. Nabrit stand outside the Supreme Court on the day of their victory in Brown v. Board of Education. *Marshall won appointment to the Supreme Court in 1967.*

branches of the NAACP had already brought into federal court antisegregation suits against school systems in five different states. Marshall combined the arguments underlying all five suits into one case: *Oliver Brown et al v. the Board of Education of Topeka, Kansas.* As Marshall designed the case, it would ask the Supreme Court to overturn the 1896 *Plessy v. Ferguson* decision that had sanctioned segregation on the grounds that public facilities that were "separate" for the races were constitutional as long as they were "equal."

From the outset, a majority of the Court favored overturning the notorious *Plessy*, but Chief Justice Earl Warren wanted a unanimous decision, so that opponents of integration would find no reason to continue their opposition. Finally, after months of deft persuasion, Warren prevailed on his colleagues. On May 17, 1954, the Supreme Court handed down its momentous ruling in *Brown v. Board of Education.* Warren read the court's decision:

> Does segregation of children in public schools solely on the basis of race, even though the physical facilities and other "tangible" factors may be equal, deprive children of the minority group of equal educational opportunities? We believe that it does. . . . We conclude that in the field of public education the doctrine of "separate but equal" has no place. Separate educational facilities are inherently unequal.

With its ruling, the Supreme Court invalidated segregation, paving the way for equal rights for all Americans.

The Struggle Continues

Now all eyes in the nation turned to the South. Would its leaders comply and desegregate their educational systems? Several border states did so immediately: Delaware, Kentucky, Maryland, Missouri, Oklahoma, and West Virginia. But throughout the following year, discouraging rumblings emanated from the Deep South, which refused to comply with the *Brown* ruling.

One year after the *Brown* decision, the Supreme Court ruled on another NAACP suit, one designed to force southern schools to obey the order to desegregate. Much to the disappointment of the black community, the Supreme Court did not demand obedience from southern states but instead declared that school systems need only show a "prompt and reasonable start towards full compliance" and that desegregation proceed "with all deliberate speed." The words were so vague as to be undefinable. Earl Warren later revealed he had been forced to compromise on the enforcement of the *Brown* case in order to obtain the unanimous vote he had originally wanted. Furthermore, Warren realized he was working at odds with the executive branch of the government. President Eisenhower regretted his appointment of Warren to the Supreme Court, later calling it "the biggest damn fool mistake I ever made." In addition, he offered no support to the principle of desegregation, privately saying that "the fellow who tries to tell me you can do these things by force is just plain nuts."

But in September 1957, the federal government finally intervened in the South on behalf of school desegregation in Little Rock, Arkansas, a racially moderate town that planned to integrate its Central High School by admitting nine black students when school resumed after the summer recess that year. This design probably would have suceeded had it not been implemented on the eve of a state gubernatorial election. The incumbent candidate, Governor Orval Faubus, saw the desegregation of Central High as an opportunity to butter up his most conservative constituents.

Faubus appeared on television the night before school opened and declared he could not guarantee the safety of the nine black students. Racists heard his announcement as an invitation to stir up trouble. Indeed, they staged violent protests outside Central High for weeks. Faubus did nothing to protect the nine black teenagers and, in fact, called out the National Guard to help block their entrance into the school building. A

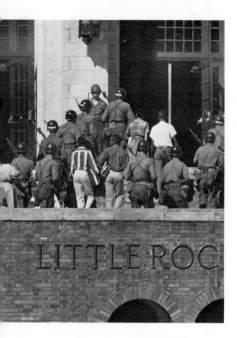

In September 1957, black students enter Little Rock Central High School flanked by federal troops.

federal district judge ordered these troops to disband, but a white mob quickly replaced them. This act of defiance finally galvanized President Eisenhower into action and on September 24, he ordered the 101st Airborne Division of the United States Army into Little Rock to protect the black students.

The Minister of Montgomery

The desegregation movement spread out from the schools and soon encompassed other public facilities, namely transportation. In December 1955, Rosa Parks, a black seamstress living in Montgomery, Alabama, refused to yield her seat on a bus to a white man. Unable to make her move, the bus driver summoned a police officer and had Rosa Parks arrested.

E. D. Nixon, head of the local branch of the NAACP—in which Parks was an active member—saw her arrest as a golden opportunity to challenge the city's Jim Crow bus laws. A former Pullman porter, Nixon had once been a member of the union led by A. Philip Randolph. In Demember 1955, Nixon summoned the leaders of the black community to a meeting to plot a citywide boycott of the bus lines as a means of protesting Jim Crow laws. They demanded the city integrate its buses and hire more black drivers.

Nixon searched for the ideal leader of the boycott and selected a young minister who had recently moved into the city, Martin Luther King, Jr. At first, King was uncertain he wanted to take part in the campaign, but Nixon insisted. He argued that because King was new to the community he could act more freely than others who had been forced to make compromises. Besides, Nixon told him, "I've already told everyone to meet at your church tonight."

The boycott began—and lasted more than a year, as black citizens walked rather than ride the buses. The economic drain on the city was so great that city leaders finally caved in and agreed to a compromise. Then the federal courts intervened and struck down the city's Jim Crow transportation laws. The boycott ended in complete victory and its leader, Martin Luther King, Jr., was elevated to national prominence at the age of 26.

King was born in 1929, the son of a Baptist minister, and was raised in a middle-class black community in Atlanta, Georgia. A scholarly, introverted youth, he entered Morehouse College in Atlanta at age 15. He graduated with honors four years later, then headed north to study first at Crozer Theological Seminary in Pennsylvania and later at Boston University, where he received a Ph.D. in theology in 1955. During his tenure at Boston University he met and married a woman who would herself become a leader in the movement for civil rights, Coretta Scott King.

King's studies in Boston had introduced him to the teachings of Mohandas Gandhi, a politician and spiritual leader in India. Gandhi had led fellow Indians in their struggle for independence against the colonial British throughout the 1930s and 1940s. King saw many parallels between the battle being waged by blacks in the United States and that fought by Indians several decades earlier. He admired Gandhi's doctrine of nonviolent resistance to oppression and emulated Gandhi's belief in *Satyagraha* (soul force) as a means of opposing social injustice.

King eventually would write that blacks must reach a point where they could tell whites: "We will not hate you, but will not obey your evil laws. We will soon wear you down by pure capacity to suffer." While still a student, King had also read the works of Henry David Thoreau, a giant of 19th-century American literature and thought, and found himself intrigued by Thoreau's ideas about civil disobedience as a means of protest. In 1960, King began to put his principles into action. He left Montgomery for a pulpit in Atlanta, Georgia, and during that year founded the Southern Christian Leadership Conference (SCLC), an organization dedicated to nonviolent protest against segregation.

In March 1956, Martin Luther King, Jr., and his wife Coretta Scott King stand amid a cheering crowd during the Montgomery bus boycott.

The Sit-In Movement and Freedom Rides

Soon the black community began staging peaceful acts of civil disobedience, both in conjunction with King and independently of him. On February 1, 1960, four black freshmen from the Negro Agricultural and Technical College in Greensboro, North Carolina, decided to challenge segregation near their campus.

After a night's planning in their college dorm rooms, the students took seats at the whites-only lunch counter at Woolworth's Department Store. They sat there all day until the store closed. The next day they came back with more people. In a matter of days dozens of students, including some whites, joined the sit-in. They encountered violence and insult and attracted national attention. They refused to move until, finally, Greensboro officials agreed to begin desegregating public facilities.

The sit-in movement spread rapidly across the South as blacks continued their challenge to segregation. In April 1960, black college students—inspired by the success of their Greensboro comrades—met in Raleigh, North Carolina, to form the Student Nonviolent Coordinating Committee (SNCC). SNCC members embarked upon a two-front campaign of nonviolent direct action: sit-ins, picketing, and boycotts; and voter registration drives. The organization, which capitalized on the youthful energy and optimism of its members, became a powerful force within the civil rights movement of the 1960s and rejected guidance offered by either Martin Luther King and his SCLC or the NAACP.

In 1961, the SNCC, SCLC, and the NAACP were joined in their desegregation efforts by the Congress of Racial Equality (CORE), an integrated civil rights organization created in 1942. The Congress sponsored a series of "Freedom Rides" on Trailways and Greyhound buses from Washington, D.C., to Jackson, Mississippi, and New Orleans, Louisiana. The Freedom Riders' goal was to challenge segregated bus seating, bus station facilities, waiting rooms, lavatories, lunch counters, and drinking fountains.

CORE had first attempted Freedom Rides in 1947,

but without success. Now the time was ripe. In May 1961, black and white Freedom Riders led by CORE's James Farmer and the SNCC's John Lewis left Washington on two buses. They encountered no trouble until they neared Anniston, Alabama, where hostile whites stood on a highway just outside of town, awaiting the first bus. One among the group threw a fire bomb into a bus window, and as the Freedom Riders came out amid billowing black smoke, the mob beat them mercilessly. One of the white Freedom Riders sustained brain damage. The outrages against the Freedom Riders continued in other cities and prompted angry intervention from the Kennedy administration, which sought first to stop the rides and ended up providing police protection for them.

In 1961 freedom riders escape from their bus after it was set afire by a group of hostile whites in Anniston, Alabama.

Albany and Birmingham

In November 1961, the SNCC pushed on in the brave spirit of the Freedom Rides and launched a desegregation and voter registration campaign in Albany, Georgia. Its enthusiastic but ill-conceived project nearly caused the civil rights movement to disband. Organizers rushed into Albany without advance planning and began their demonstrations and marches. Local ministers asked Martin Luther King to join in the protests there, and King was ultimately arrested and jailed. In order to prevent King's arrest from becoming a nationally celebrated cause, the local sheriff, Laurie Pritchett, raised money within the white community for King's bail.

When King returned from jail, he found that the Albany Movement had disintegrated into a competition between warring factions of black protest leaders: The young radicals of the SNCC, the older and more staid members of the NAACP, and the black churches all regarded each other with suspicion and vied for the control of the civil rights movement. Furthermore, the Albany Movement attracted no broad base of support, thanks to the shrewd strategies of Laurie Pritchett, who had studied King's work. Pritchett knew that although

King's movement was nonviolent, it nevertheless relied on confrontations with the police—and these he refused to provide. He ordered his entire force to treat the protesters gently, thus denying them any opportunity to gain media attention and national recognition for their efforts. Never again would King or other civil rights leaders act without careful advance planning.

The Albany debacle set the stage for dramatic confrontations in Birmingham, Alabama, during the spring of 1963. Birmingham's notorious commissioner of public safety, T. Eugene "Bull" Connor, was not inclined toward gentility with black protesters. He was determined to block their attempts at desegregation in every possible way. After the setback in Albany, King and the SCLC moved into Birmingham knowing they would have to score a victory or face the dissolution of the civil rights movement. King was determined to provoke a confrontation in Birmingham and capture the attention of the American public. Bull Connor was all too willing to oblige him in this effort.

On April 12, 1963, King led a march on the Birmingham city hall and was arrested. While in jail, he wrote "A Letter from a Birmingham Jail," his response to a letter that white clergymen had addressed to King and published in the local newspaper. These men of the cloth had urged King not to create a national crisis over the issue of civil rights for blacks.

King penned his eloquent response on scrap paper and had it smuggled out of the jail. He argued that Afro-Americans could no longer wait for rights that should have been theirs centuries ago. King justified civil disobedience by showing it was the only way blacks could overturn unjust laws because they were barred from full participation in the political process. He claimed they had a moral responsibility not to obey immoral laws. His eloquent words moved a nation of white moderates to embrace his position.

In May, King hit upon the idea of using high school students in his demonstrations. This decision met with widespread criticism from within the movement; nevertheless, it worked. The nation watched in stunned horror as Bull Connor turned fire hoses and unleashed police dogs on thousands of black teenage protest marchers. The news footage of the dogs tearing at the demonstrators and of people being swept away by the torrent of water shocked and moved white Americans. President Kennedy said the pictures made him sick— but still claimed he lacked a constitutional mandate to act on behalf of the demonstrators.

The violence in Birmingham stirred black Americans to further action. More arrests followed "The Children's Crusade." This time in addition to police dogs and fire hoses Bull Connor sent in tanks. Several days later negotiations with embarrassed white leaders brought a promise to desegregate public facilities and the Birmingham campaign ended in victory.

That summer, flushed with success, black leaders planned a massive protest rally in Washington over the lack of government action in civil rights. The more conservative organizations, such as the NAACP and National Urban League, had before shied away from such a protest march in the nation's capital fearing the violence it might provoke. But after witnessing the terrible police brutality in Birmingham, they joined in the planning. The Kennedy administration attempted to block the march, but failing to do so they instead sought to guide its course.

The March on Washington for Jobs and Freedom drew national attention. Approximately 250,000 people came to Washington on August 28, 1963. Protesters anxiously awaited the speech of SNCC representative John Lewis. He planned to criticize the federal government for its failure to enforce the *Brown* decision and the Kennedy administration for failing to fulfill its promises on civil rights. At the last minute, the administration was able to persuade Lewis to moderate his speech.

But the historic moment of the event arrived when Martin Luther King ascended the platform to say a few words of his own. His 15-minute speech, echoing the refrain "I have a dream," stirred both the crowd and the nation and gave him an indelible place in history.

Members of the Birmingham, Alabama, fire department turn their hoses on a crowd of civil rights protesters in 1963.

Toward Federal Legislation

The events in Birmingham, the stirring March on Washington, and the November assassination of John F. Kennedy, who had slowly begun to embrace civil rights, combined to impel Congress toward the passage of the Civil Rights Act of 1964, the most sweeping civil rights legislation since Reconstruction. It outlawed discrimination on the basis of race, religion, or sex in all places of public access and in those supported by federal tax dollars; authorized the attorney general to hasten the process of school desegregation by bringing suits to court; strengthened voting rights laws; established the Equal Opportunity Commission to abolish all job discrimination; and gave federal agencies the power to withhold funds from state-administered programs that discriminated against blacks.

The year 1964 proved a watershed, too, in the registration of black voters by the SNCC, which launched the Mississippi Freedom Summer that year. The SNCC targeted Mississippi because only 5 percent of the state's eligible black voters were registered, the fewest of any state in the nation. At first the SNCC intended to bar whites from participation in the campaign, so strong had antiwhite sentiment become within the organization.

It was finally decided, however, that the presence of thousands of white college students in the Deep South would publicize the drive and also protect it from local police who, it was certain, would not harm the children of the white middle class. SNCC leaders underestimated their enemies. On June 22, SNCC leaders received word that three young civil rights workers—two white, one black—were missing in rural Mississippi. The eventual disclosure of their death outraged the nation.

In 1965 the campaign for voter registration shifted its focus to Selma, Alabama, and its leadership to Martin Luther King, who had won the Nobel Peace Prize in 1964. Of the Selma campaign, King said on January 2, 1965, "We will dramatize the situation to arouse the federal government by marching by the thousands to the places of registration. . . . We are not asking, we are demanding the ballot."

The local sheriff in Selma, James Clark, was already infamous to those within the movement for the vicious and violent manner in which his men treated civil rights workers. Within a month of their arrival in Selma, 2,000 people had been arrested, and the news media began focusing on the brutality of Selma's police. Organizers decided to address their grievances about Clark and his men to George Wallace, Alabama's governor.

On Sunday, March 7, the protesters began the 50-mile walk from Selma to Montgomery. As they approached the Edmund Pettus Bridge, leading out of town, the marchers found their way blocked by both the Alabama state police and Clark's men. The officers attacked them viciously, some charging through the crowd on horseback and wielding electric cattle prods. Others swung their nightsticks, clubbing even the children in the crowd. The nation witnessed this sickening scene on broadcast news and responded as it never had. Thousands of people from all over the country flooded into Alabama to participate in the massive protest march from Selma to Montgomery. The nation was properly indignant over the blatant brutality of "Bloody Sunday."

On March 21, 3,000 people marched from Selma to Montgomery. President Lyndon Johnson called out the Alabama National Guard to protect them. On the outskirts of Montgomery they were joined by King and 30,000 others. The two groups made their way to the state capitol where speaker after speaker denounced violence and racism and called for a voting rights campaign and crusades against poverty and segregated schools. In the stunned aftermath of Selma, Congress passed the Voting Rights Act of 1965, which provided federally supervised voter registration in the South. Thousands of blacks registered and eventually voted and brought to fruition the seed work done by the SNCC during its voter registration drives. The civil rights movement had reached its zenith. ≈

On the second march from Selma, Alabama, to the state capitol in Montgomery, civil rights sympathizers turned out by the thousands and completed their route with the protection of the National Guard.

In July 1968, members of the Black Panther party march along 42nd Street in New York City in order to protest the murder trial of Panther "defense minister" Huey P. Newton.

BLACK NATIONALISM AND BEYOND

Unlike their counterparts in the South, northern blacks could not revel in the demise of Jim Crow, because they had never been subject to legislated discrimination. In the North, blacks enjoyed free access to public transportation, polling places, and other facilities. Yet they, too, suffered white racism and were shunted into inferior urban schools, denied access to higher-paying jobs, and trapped in urban slums. In northern cities, however, this form of segregation was insidious; it existed everywhere but was not written into law.

Many Afro-Americans in the North expressed skepticism about the goal of a racially integrated society. They knew firsthand that greater intermingling between whites and blacks did not necessarily end either racism or, more importantly, the poverty endemic to black communities. Many ghetto dwellers, especially the young, viewed with disdain Martin Luther King's pleas for reconciliation between the races. They adopted a stance far more radical than King's, arguing that blacks should remove themselves from the society of whites and demand an equal share of political power—meeting white violence with retaliatory violence of their own. Afro-Americans espousing this na-

On the 21st anniversary of the Brown *decision, supporters of school desegregation march in Boston.*

tionalist philosophy turned for leadership to a black man many regarded as the antithesis of Martin Luther King, Jr., Malcolm X.

Malcolm X

Born Malcolm Little in 1925, he was the son of a West Indian mother and Afro-American father, a preacher who died at the hands of a white mob in Lansing, Michigan. This death splintered the family, and Malcolm was placed in the foster care of a white couple. He later recalled them with bitterness, telling an interviewer, "My presence in that home was like a cat or a parrot or any type of pet they had." After finishing the eighth grade, Malcolm dropped out of school and ran away first to Boston and later to Harlem, where he supported himself working as both a bookie and a bootlegger. His seedy career ended abruptly in 1946, when he was arrested for burglary and sentenced to 10 years in jail.

During his prison term, Malcolm experienced a spiritual redemption through exposure to the teachings of Elijah Muhammad, founder of a religious sect called the Nation of Islam, or the Black Muslims. Muhammad advocated a rejection of the white culture imposed on blacks by the institution of slavery. He denounced the adoption of Christianity, white surnames, and the identity of "so-called American Negroes." His radical doctrine appealed to Malcolm Little, who accepted it as his own, replacing his last name (that conferred on his ancestors by white slave owners) with an X.

By the time of his release from prison in 1952, Malcolm X had joined Elijah Muhammad's ministry. For the next 13 years he preached to a growing following, championing black nationalism and the embracing of African culture and heritage. His militant sermons drew fire from whites, who accused him of "inflaming" ghetto resentments. He also met with disapproval from Elijah Muhammad in 1963 and was suspended from the Black Muslims. In response, Malcolm X founded the rival Muslim Mosque, Inc. and in February 1965 was assassinated by three men claiming to be Black Muslims. However, historians still debate the identity of these killers.

Malcolm X and Martin Luther King, Jr.—one a Black Muslim leader and a survivor of ghetto poverty, the other a Christian clergyman from a middle-class Atlanta family—represented two significant but differing views about American racial problems. King advocated integration, Malcolm X urged voluntary separation from whites. He said the only thing he liked integrated was coffee, which he took with milk. King advocated Christian love and nonviolence. Malcolm X dismissed this "passivity" as foolish and urged his followers to counter racist violence with violence of their own, telling a Harlem crowd: "I don't believe we're going to overcome by singing. If you're going to get yourself a .45 and start singing 'We Shall Overcome' [the hymn of the civil rights movement], I'm with you." After Malcolm X's death, his separatist philosophy was perpetuated by black nationalist organizations such as the Black Panther Party, founded in 1966 in Oakland,

Malcolm X addresses a Harlem rally in 1963.

California, by Huey Newton and Bobby Seale. The following year, at a conference in Newark, New Jersey, the Panthers called for "the partitioning of the United States into two separate independent nations, one to be a homeland for white and the other to be a homeland for black Americans."

The Cities Riot

Six months after Malcolm X's death, the violence characterizing the Long Hot Summers began. In August 1965 urban blacks—whose rage Malcolm X had so eloquently voiced—rioted for five days in the Los Angeles neighborhood of Watts. Some 50,000 Afro-Americans looted stores, attacked whites and police, and burned buildings, until they were brought under the control of 1,500 Los Angeles Police and 14,000 National Guardsmen. In all, the fury injured 900 people and took 34 lives. Police, who arrested a total of 4,000 people during the days that chaos reigned in Watts, termed the upheaval an insurrection. There were many more to come.

As Americans stared in disbelief at the televised news reports of the Watts conflagration, Chicago, too, erupted in riot. On August 12, a black woman was run over by a truck from an all-white fire station. The incident set off two days and nights of looting and arson. In the summer of 1965, urban blacks across the country turned to violence in their frustration with racism and

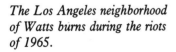

The Los Angeles neighborhood of Watts burns during the riots of 1965.

In July 1966, National Guardsmen with bayonets push rioting blacks away from a burning building in Detroit.

poverty. A year later, similar scenes of looting, burning, and arrest were repeated in Atlanta, Georgia; Chicago, Illinois; Omaha, Nebraska; the Michigan cities of Lansing and Benton Harbor; and the Ohio cities of Dayton and Cleveland.

The Long Hot Summers of 1965 and 1966 were a mere prelude to the summer of 1967, when the United States witnessed the most destructive wave of racial violence in its history. Riots swept through 100 cities, including Newark, New Jersey, a town plagued by the nation's highest crime rate, highest percentage of black unemployment, and greatest number of condemned residential buildings. In July 1967, the arrest of a black Newark cab driver incited violence so bloody that New Jersey's governor Richard Hughes called it a city "in open rebellion." In all, 25 people were killed, 1,200 wounded, 1,300 arrested; and the city sustained property damages amounting to more than $10 million.

As Newark burned, the worst race riot in American history besieged Detroit, Michigan—then one of the most racially progressive cities in the United States. Blacks constituted almost half the city's elected officials, who had recently won a federal grant in order to implement antipoverty and urban renewal programs. Michigan's booming auto industry provided well-paying jobs to many workers. Two-thirds of all black families owned cars and half lived in their own homes during an era when more than one-third of all black families lived below the poverty level. Yet this relative prosperity was marred by a strained relationship between Detroit blacks and the predominantly white local police force, often accused of racially motivated police brutality.

On the night of July 18, 1967, the Detroit police arrested 18 young blacks at a nightclub on the charge that they were selling liquor illegally. The incident ignited 6 days of vicious rioting, in which 4,000 separate fires gutted 1,300 buildings. About 5,000 blacks lost their homes as the fires spread throughout the city. In all, Detroit withstood $250 million in property loss. Poorly trained National Guardsmen panicked and fired into houses and commercial buildings in an effort to stop the looting and protect themselves from snipers. Their indiscriminate gunshots left 43 people dead. As in previous years, the violence spread from one locale to many across America, taking 90 lives before the Long Hot Summer of 1967 finally came to a close.

A Time of Reflection

In 1965, President Lyndon Johnson sought to understand the causes of the violence rocking the United States and appointed a National Advisory Commission on Civil Disorders, naming Otto Kerner, a former governor of Ohio, as chairman. The Kerner Commission issued a report in 1968 and startled the public by placing the blame for the rioting not on the participants, but on racism: "White society is deeply implicated in the ghetto. White institutions created it, white institutions maintained it, and white society condoned it." The report recommended sweeping social changes to alleviate the plight of the ghetto dweller and warned: "We are moving toward two societies, one black, one white—separate and unequal."

The riots jarred not only white Americans, but also moderate blacks such as Martin Luther King, Jr. By

1967, King had broadened the purpose of his integration movement—fighting, too, for political and economic equality for blacks. King's rhetoric now reflected the increased militancy of Afro-Americans across the country, and he publicly addressed not only American domestic policies, but also international affairs. In particular, King voiced his objection to the Vietnam War, stating as early as 1965, "The long night of war must be stopped."

King's stand against the war in Vietnam cost him support from within the remnants of the civil rights movement. To regain lost momentum, in 1968, he planned a nationwide campaign to dramatize the realities of economic injustice in the wealthiest nation in the world. But on April 3, King embarked on a fateful trip to Memphis, Tennessee, to address a crowd of striking

Hosea Williams, Jesse Jackson, and the Reverend Ralph Abernathy, (left to right) stand with Martin Luther King, Jr., on the balcony where King was slain a day later.

sanitation workers, hoping to quell the violence resulting from their walkout. That night he gave his last speech, telling his audience about recent threats on his own life:

> But it doesn't matter with me now. Because I've been to the mountaintop. I don't mind. Like anybody, I would like to live a long life. Longevity has its place. But I'm not concerned about that now. I just want to do God's will. And He's allowed me to go up to the mountain! And I've looked over and I've seen the promised land! I may not get there with you, but I want you to know tonight that we as a people will get to the promised land. And I am happy tonight! I'm not worried about anything! I'm not fearing any man! Mine eyes have seen the glory of the coming of the Lord!

The next evening, King fell to white assassin James Earl Ray as he was standing on the balcony of the Lorraine Motel in Memphis. Once again, when word of King's death reached black communities across the country, the ghettos erupted in flames. On April 9, more than 300,000 people of all races marched behind King's coffin as it was pulled through the streets of

In 1971 black soldiers in Long Binh, Vietnam, observe the birthday of Martin Luther King, Jr.

Atlanta on a farm wagon drawn by two Georgia mules. Afro-Americans mourned not only King himself, but also the fading civil rights movement, which lost its momentum in the aftermath of King's death.

A Changing Community

Those within the civil rights movement took various paths in the years following King's murder, many assuming public office. The ranks of black elected officials swelled in 1968, when a record number of black men and the first black woman representative—Shirley Chisholm—were elected to Congress. The 10 Afro-Americans in Congress that year topped a previous record of 8 who had sat in the 44th Congress of 1875–77.

Afro-Americans continued to win votes throughout the 1970s and 1980s and made a particularly strong showing in mayoral elections in the country's major cities: In 1973 Detroit elected Coleman Young mayor and Los Angeles first voted Tom Bradley into its executive office; in 1981 former U.S. representative to the United Nations Andrew Young assumed the office of mayor in Atlanta; and in 1983 Chicago boosted Mayor Harold Washington to power. Despite the number of black elected officials, however, no single individual approached the stature of Martin Luther King until Jesse Jackson, a former member of King's inner circle, won several Democratic presidential primaries in 1988.

Jesse Jackson

Born in Greenville, South Carolina, in 1941, Jesse Jackson began his work in civil rights in 1965. In that year, as a student at Chicago Theological Seminary, he traveled to Selma, Alabama, in order to learn firsthand about Martin Luther King and the Southern Christian Leadership Conference. The young seminarian soon earned an important role in the SCLC and during the next three years established the movement's base in Chicago. After King's death in 1968, Jackson went on

In October 1987, Jesse Jackson announces his candidacy for the presidency of the United States.

to establish his own Chicago-based organizations, first directing Operation Breadbasket—which offered marketing and management services to minority-owned businesses—and later, in 1971, founding People United to Save Humanity (PUSH). As the director of PUSH he won almost $5 million in grants from the federal government and channeled the money into innovative inner-city public school programs for young blacks. Jackson remembered all too keenly the racism he knew as a boy growing up in South Carolina and wanted to spare young Afro-Americans that hardship. He told an interviewer: "[On] Saturdays I'd sell peanuts and soft drinks at the stadium. Whites sat all around drinking liquor. They'd say all kinds of vulgar things, call me nigger, try to shortchange me. . . . I couldn't go to the front at the movies, I couldn't use the bathrooms. It was humiliating."

For the next decade, Jackson worked within PUSH and other grass roots organizations, but in 1984 he entered the mainstream of American politics by launching a candidacy for that year's presidential election. Jackson forged a diverse constituency he dubbed the Rainbow Coalition. Although he won only one primary, he established himself as the leading Afro-American politician of his day and laid the groundwork for his next presidential campaign. He later recalled: "In 1984 my basic challenge was to open up the [Democratic] party to be fair. And I put a lot of focus on the Voting Rights Act. In 1984 we were encountering so much hostility—from the party, from the media—we had to spend a lot more time fighting for honor, fighting for dignity." Despite opposition from within the party, Jackson remained a loyal Democrat and registered 2 million new voters, many of whom cast their ballots for Democratic candidates in later elections. "I sit on the stage now," Jackson proclaimed, "and no one can challenge my Democratic Party credentials."

During the 1988 Democratic primaries, Jackson emerged as a serious contender for the nomination, winning a majority of the delegates in Michigan, the District of Columbia, his home state of North Carolina, and in other states in the Deep South. White voters as well as blacks jumped on the Jackson bandwagon and boosted him to national prominence.

Jackson's Rainbow Coalition united disparate factions within the black community. He spoke for the black middle class that had burgeoned as a result of Martin Luther King's movement for integration. He offered hope to the inner-city blacks who had been left behind in the ghettos. But Jackson also voiced the wishes and fears of an even broader segment of American society. In 1988, a white voter expressed the views of many in *Time* magazine: "I'm drawn to a candidate I believe in, someone who could possibly carry out the goals and ideals I found in the '60s. [Jackson's] talking about . . . drugs and economic devastation, issues that transcend ethnic and religious problems." Thus, in 1988 Jesse Jackson seemed to realize the dreams of generations of Afro-Americans, who—in the words of Martin Luther King, Jr.—saw Jackson judged not by the color of his skin but by the content of his character.

FURTHER READING

Anderson, Jervis. *This Was Harlem: 1900–1950*. New York: Farrar, Straus & Giroux, 1981.

Baldwin, James. *The Fire Next Time*. New York: Dial Press, 1963.

Franklin, John Hope, and Alfred Moss, Jr. *From Slavery to Freedom*. 6th ed. New York: Knopf, 1980.

Franklin, John Hope, and August Meier. *Black Leaders of the Twentieth Century*. Urbana: University of Illinois Press, 1982.

Garrow, David J. *Bearing the Cross*. New York: Morrow, 1986.

Genovese, Eugene G. *Roll, Jordan, Roll*. New York: Pantheon, 1976.

Litwack, Leon F., and August Meier. *Black Leaders of the Nineteenth Century*. Urbana: University of Illinois, 1988.

Meier, August, and Elliot Rudwick. *From Plantation to Ghetto*. 3rd ed. New York: Hill and Wang, 1976.

Smead, Howard. *Blood Justice: The Lynching of Mack Charles Parker*. New York: Oxford University Press, 1986.

Williams, Juan. *Eyes on the Prize*. New York: Penguin, 1987.

Williamson, Joel. *Rage for Order*. New York: Oxford University Press, 1986.

Woodward, C. Vann. *The Strange Career of Jim Crow*. 3rd ed. New York: Oxford University Press, 1974.

Wright, Richard. *Native Son*. 1940. Reprint. New York: Harper & Row, 1969.

INDEX

PICTURE CREDITS

HOWARD SMEAD is a lecturer in History and Afro-American studies at the University of Maryland and the director of night research at the *Washington Post*. He is the author of *Blood Justice: The Lynching of Mack Charles Parker* and *The Redneck Waltz*.

DANIEL PATRICK MOYNIHAN is the senior United States senator from New York. He is also the only person in American history to serve in the cabinets or subcabinets of four successive presidents—Kennedy, Johnson, Nixon, and Ford. Formerly a professor of government at Harvard University, he has written and edited many books, including *Beyond the Melting Pot, Ethnicity: Theory and Experience* (both with Nathan Glazer), *Loyalties,* and *Family and Nation.*